THRIVING
ON OUR
DIFFERENCES

THRIVING
ON OUR
DIFFERENCES

BY KAREN LYNN DAVIDSON

Deseret Book Company
Salt Lake City, Utah

Library of Congress Cataloging-in-Publication Data

Davidson, Karen Lynn.
    Thriving on our differences / by Karen Lynn Davidson.
      p. cm.
    Includes index.
    ISBN 0-87579-359-2
    1. Women, Mormon. I. Title.
BX8641.D33   1990
248.8′43 — dc20

                                 90-40866
                                      CIP

Printed in the United States of America

10   9   8   7   6   5   4   3   2   1

To the thousands of Latter-day Saint women it has been my pleasure to know. Thank you for your company, your good humor, and your example. You always make sure that charity never fails and the hours never drag.

Contents

CHAPTER ONE

Insider/Outsider

Many Latter-day Saint women—probably most of us—go through times when we feel that we don't fit in with the rest of the people in our ward. Generally we are able to take those feelings in stride. In a short while, as soon as we get to know people better, or as soon as a few more kindred spirits move into the ward, we find that we are more comfortable.

But for some women the feeling of alienation can be deeper and much longer lasting. As a sense of estrangement and aloneness builds up week by week, a woman may finally decide that her participation in her ward is nothing but routine and pretense. Convinced that she will never feel accepted, she sees no point in continuing to attend meetings where she feels unwelcome or out of touch. She becomes part of the rolls of the less active, that list of people who now choose to stay home but who at one time believed (or at least their families did) that The Church of Jesus Christ of Latter-day Saints represented for them hope, socialization, and a divine plan for their earthly happiness and eternal salvation. They become the names with no faces on the ward

1

list, known personally only to a patient home teacher or a dutiful visiting teacher.

When a woman reaches the point of thinking "this isn't for me—there is nothing for me here, and I don't belong here," everyone loses. The Church loses the opportunity to share its teachings and opportunities with a daughter of our Father in Heaven; the local ward loses the friendship and talents of a sister; and the woman has cut herself off from the fulfillment and joy that are potentially hers as an active member of her ward.

My aim in this book is to prevent that tragic parting of the ways. This book is not a problem-solving manual, nor is it just a naive "let's-all-be-more-cheerful" book. Its purpose is to remind us that sisterhood does not mean sameness, that commitment does not mean uniformity, and that women of vastly different outlooks and backgrounds can still share a joyful and enriching association as Latter-day Saints.

The reasons a woman might feel alienated, even to the point of opting out of Church activity, are not exactly the same for any two women. But over and over again, certain circumstances or attitudes seem to be at the root. This book focuses on five of the usual situations that might cause women to feel out of the Latter-day Saint mainstream: the single woman, who faces the problem of being "single in a married Church"; the woman who joined the Church or returned to activity only recently and who feels she can never truly be on the same wavelength as the women who have participated for their whole lives; the woman who is rearing her children alone or who is the mother or step-mother of a blended family (this woman has a family, but it does not correspond to the image of the traditional family); the woman who is married to a man who is not a Latter-day Saint or to a less-active Latter-day Saint husband and who therefore faces the task of pursuing her Church callings and activity without her husband at her side; and the woman who is a wife and mother in a traditional Latter-day Saint home, who seems to have it all, but who still feels that some *other* woman, more fulfilled and contented than she is, is in fact at the real center of things.

Why am I qualified to write this book? Not through any professional training as a psychologist or counselor. My background is in literature (which, frankly, I have always considered quite good training in understanding the quirks and foibles of human nature), and I have spent many years speaking with and observing women in the Church. As a faculty member at Brigham Young University, I knew and spoke with many of our young women. In pondering what constitutes sisterhood and how we can express our individuality in the context of our sisterhood, I am drawing on conversations, readings, and insights gathered over many years.

Undoubtedly my most important qualification is that I myself am an outsider in many ways. I fit into many of the outsider groups I will be discussing. I am a walking, talking, life-size visual aid for the points I am making, a visual aid that says, "The Church of Jesus Christ of Latter-day Saints can accommodate — in fact, can benefit from — the active participation of many different kinds of women." The umbrella of the Church is a big one; it can welcome and protect many different kinds of women. I've found warmth and friendship there for decades now, and I feel sad when I meet women who don't feel there is any way they can find those same opportunities. I hope in some way this book can help.

Just so you'll know, here are some of the specific ways in which I don't fit the usual pattern for Latter-day Saint women:

I was single until I was thirty-eight years old. Needless to say, that does not fit the usual LDS timetable. Furthermore—and this is where a few people begin to raise their eyebrows in shock—I enjoyed those thirty-eight years very much.

When I did finally marry, I married a man who had been married before. He is a wonderful husband, I love being married, I acquired some wonderful stepsons, and we've had some great times together, but we still don't meet the traditional Latter-day Saint definition of family. Marrying a divorced man doesn't violate any laws. What it does violate is tradition.

I have no children of my own. Womanhood and motherhood are so often equated in our Church that not being a mother is a big distancer from the norm. Motherhood is often described as a woman's greatest mission, and it's a mission I haven't filled biologically.

I can't sew. I am emotionally allergic to that rustling sound a dress pattern makes when you take it out of the envelope. When Ulysses left for the Trojan wars and was absent from home for twenty years and presumed dead, his faithful wife Penelope kept hordes of rowdy suitors at bay by telling them, "I cannot consider an offer of marriage until I finish weaving this shroud for my aged father-in-law." Every day she would weave, and every night she would secretly undo the day's weaving. The weaving served its purpose by remaining unfinished. I too have a piece of Penelope-work, a needlepoint seat cover that I began about ten years ago. Every couple of years I get it out and attempt to work on it, just to reassure myself that maybe I could be a needle-woman if I wanted to. Like Penelope's shroud, my needlepoint serves its purpose by remaining unfinished.

Nor am I famous for my cooking skills. When one of my stepsons asks, "Is this homemade?" he is hoping the answer is no. We are better off with things straight from a box or can. On the other hand, my husband is a superb cook. He is also very artistic, with an excellent eye for interior design, flower arranging, and table settings. It is wonderful to be married to someone with those skills. The drawback is that these talents, because they are his rather than mine, only contribute to our image as the Odd Couple of our ward.

So I represent some great divergences from the norm, and I'm sure that sometimes when I have moved to a new ward I have been viewed at least initially as a suspicious character. My Church experience has taken me all the way from Cambridge Branch in Cambridge, England, where I was given four callings almost the minute I walked in the door, to Pleasant View Sixth Ward in Provo, Utah, where there were not enough callings to go around. Sometimes I had to wait awhile to attain any kind of credibility, especially in the bigger wards. Other times, for instance in England and in Irving Second Ward in Texas, they were so glad to have someone to fill several vacant callings that they were willing to suspend all suspicion and just audition me on the job, so to speak.

Each experience has added to my understanding. As the years go by, I understand more and judge less. In our day, women in vastly differing circumstances are members of the Lord's kingdom as his Latter-day Saint daughters, and two women who have virtually nothing in common except their desire to be faithful keepers of his covenants may have equally valid claims on the blessings of gospel living and Church membership.

No matter what her personal circumstances or her current Church assignment may be, every Latter-day Saint woman age eighteen and over is a member of the Relief Society. All active members of the Relief Society tend to share certain ideals and goals, but within those ideals is a great deal of room for individuality. Certainly the history of the Relief Society shows it to be an organization designed not to exclude nor to limit any woman but rather to encourage and celebrate the individuality and talents of each of its members. Ida Smith, formerly the director of the Women's Research Institute at BYU, noted that when the Prophet Joseph Smith organized the Relief Society in 1842 at the request of a group of Latter-day Saint women, he "taught them that they were responsible for their own salvation, that they had access to every blessing the priesthood had access to, that they had equal access to the Holy Ghost and to every spiritual gift, that they also had direct access to the Savior — to model him, to become like him, to be heirs in his kingdom.

"The Prophet removed some of the excuses afforded woman in her passive, dependent role and made her responsible for herself. In a very real way, he started the modern-day women's movement. Many of the early Mormon sisters caught his vision for women, got in the game, and ran with the ball. Women in Utah and Wyoming had the vote fifty years before women in the United States received it generally. And as we read and ponder the writings of many nineteenth-century Latter-day Saint women, we know that they knew who they were." ("A Woman's Role and Destiny," *Woman to Woman,* Salt Lake City: Deseret Book, 1986, p. 45.)

If a woman who feels like an outsider can become an accepted and happy member of her ward, everyone is better off. So who is responsible for this integration? Both sides must play a role in building bridges and removing barriers. The ward members might need to become less judgmental and suspicious, more willing to take the initiative in welcoming a new or returning member. The woman herself might need to be less defensive, less critical of herself, and more tolerant of the human frailties of the ward leaders and members.

Most of the discussion in the following chapters centers on what the woman can do rather than on what the ward members can do because I feel it is better at the outset to recognize an important truth: no one else's attitudes and actions are in your control. You can decide what you will do, but you can't decide what anyone else can do. If you feel that the day-to-day and week-to-week bond between you and the Church is strained and you wish to strengthen it to achieve a higher level of harmony and comfort, your approach, attitudes, persistence, words, and actions are in your control. No one else's are.

"But is all this really worth it?" a discouraged sister may ask. "If I get so little satisfaction out of Church activity, why shouldn't I just forget the whole thing? Why should I spend my energies trying to fit in where I don't seem to belong?" Every ward roster includes some women who are marginally active members on the discontented fringes of the organization. The ward asks very little of them; it's more or less understood that they won't accept a calling and won't fully participate. Others have even lapsed into total inactivity. The temptation just to drift into the ranks of the less active may be very strong.

Before she decides, "I'll give up because I'll never belong," I ask each woman to consider three reasons why it *is* worth it, even in times of discouragement, to maintain Church activity, to meet the ward and its members halfway — and even more than halfway:

1. It's too easy to react negatively because of a few tactless people or a few hurtful remarks. In any ward or branch, the members who are accepting, helpful, and friendly will far outnumber those who are judgmental and suspicious. Don't punish yourself and the people who want to associate with you because of a narrow-minded few. You will miss out on too much.

2. It is impossible to know what the future may bring. In a moment of spiritual discouragement, life without the Church may seem feasible; it may even seem like a relief. But burnt bridges and severed ties are hard to repair. The enduring, trustworthy, loving friendships that are one of the great blessings of Church activity may help you through a future time of tragedy or loneliness. Such friendships are not unique to the Church, of course, but hundreds of thousands of women over many decades can testify that the Church and its network of mutual support have pulled them through difficult times.

3. Beyond practical and social reasons for maintaining Church activity is the issue of the truthfulness of the gospel. Almost any member of the Church finds that a testimony is stronger at some times in life than at other times. If you want to gain a testimony or strengthen the testimony you already have, be where the spiritual influences are the strongest. Don't define it as "just going through the motions"; instead, give yourself credit for recognizing that right actions often bring faith and testimony in their wake.

What about a woman who is convinced that the Church and its leadership are inherently flawed? Anyone who expects this book to be critical of The Church of Jesus Christ of Latter-day Saints and its leaders is in for a disappointment. Although Church leaders have been known to make insensitive statements and Church programs have been known to accommodate some life situations better than others, this book will not attempt to catalogue nor correct those perceived shortcomings. It is not directly in our power to rewrite a too-rigid talk nor to do away with ward snobbishness. It is not in our power to control what others do. Each one can, however, decide what she herself will do: she can resolve to be more tolerant, she can resolve to attend her meetings, she can resolve to be a woman of good will. I do

8

not ask any woman to deny her individuality or become something less than her genuine self. But with greater sensitivity and tolerance, the breaking point — the point at which the woman decides, "I just don't fit in here; this isn't for me," or the ward decides, "We just don't know what to do with someone like her" — won't always loom just around the corner, making everyone anxious and unhappy.

If a woman feels that the Church is in some way insensitive to her needs, I am convinced that she does not help her situation when she allows that perceived insensitivity to become the main focus of her relationship with the Church. When she is fixated on the put-downs, she will miss the talks and lessons and programs that will reach out and heal. I knew a woman who watched every session of every general conference, not to receive inspiration and direction, but to keep track of how seldom the Brethren acknowledged the needs of single women. Another woman once said to me, "I know a lot of women in the Church who are really hurting. Don't you?" She was hoping for a strong and bitter agreement from me. I told her yes, I did know a lot of women in the Church who were really hurting. I also knew a lot of women outside the Church who were hurting, and a lot of women who were not hurting, both within the Church and outside it.

I am therefore not willing to point to the Church as the villain each time a Latter-day Saint woman is unhappy. Three researchers who studied the roots of depression in Latter-day Saint women presented their findings in a recent article. They discussed some statistics showing that Latter-day Saint women were not prone to depression in unusual numbers, and the authors noted the danger of attributing personal unhappiness (or even, in fact, personal happiness) to the Church:

"Very few people live without experiencing depressive

symptoms at some point in their lives. One reason depression in Utah has been attributed to religious values and norms is merely because religion becomes a factor in all aspects of life when religious involvement is heavy. It would seem wiser not to use this convenient scapegoat or, on the other hand, give total credit for one's emotional well-being to a religious institution (or any other single factor). Giving either undue blame or undue credit to the Church for the quality of one's life will not help in the difficult task of understanding and solving emotional problems." (Harry P. Bluhm, David C. Spendlove, and Dee Wayne West, "Depression in Mormon Women," *Dialogue,* Summer 1986, p. 153.)

Over the years, I have passed through varying degrees of comfort on the insider-outsider spectrum. I have found that for every remark or event in the Church that depressed me, there was a program, a friendship, a teaching, an assignment, a satisfaction that more than made up the difference. Taken all in all, in is better than out. In fact, many women in the Church find that the teachings of the Church help to focus their thinking and vitalize their creativity, providing them with a background against which they can assess the feelings and experiences that are important to them. Addressing the 1983 BYU Women's Conference, Professor Eugene England, who has studied Mormon literature for many years, stated that in his opinion "Mormon women are more free, more daring, inventive, original in thought and unique in voice than Mormon men. . . . Scanning down a select bibliography of Mormon literature I compiled lately, I find it clear that in every period and most genres more than half of our best, most challenging original work is by women." (Quoted in *Dialogues with Myself: Personal Essays on Mormon Experience,* Midvale, Utah: Orion Books, 1984, p. 154.)

Women who feel like outsiders tend to assume their

feelings are unique. Isolation overwhelms them; they feel no one could possibly understand them. But are outsiders really in the minority? We might at first assume so; an outsider is a woman by herself, on the edge, circling around the fringes of the large, secure group of women who know they belong. Theoretically, all the women in this large group at the center mingle easily in their ward meetings; they blend without stress or fuss into a new ward; they know just what to do to have beautiful homes and happy families. But here is the paradox: these women who fit in so well, who exemplify Latter-day Saint womanhood with such confidence, who never question their roles, may actually be in the minority. It's not the outsiders who turn out to be the unusual ones, in the sense of actual numbers; the outsiders, in fact, prevail, or so I am convinced after many years of observation and discussion.

Each Latter-day Saint woman who feels she is an outsider should recognize that she is not alone. Most Latter-day Saint women would, in honest discussion, acknowledge having felt alienated or distanced at some time in their lives. Women who have served the Church for decades, who have truly paid their dues in every way as faithful members and who have every reason to assume that their credibility is established, can sometimes encounter a circumstance that changes the way others view them. One woman's family was having financial difficulty because the husband's salary as a schoolteacher was not really enough to support the son and the daughter who were both serving missions in Asian countries. The husband, a member of a stake presidency, had already taken on additional part-time work. When an opportunity came along for the woman to do some part-time bookkeeping at a pharmacy within walking distance of their home, she gave thanks in her prayers that her Father in Heaven had provided this means of tiding them over during that difficult time. That's how she saw the opportunity. Imagine her astonishment when a friend told her that some ward members had critized her for "not having enough faith to stay home." The woman said, "It was clear that some ward members now had a whole new feeling about me. I was not setting a good example. The trouble was, I started imagining that most of the ward members were suddenly looking at me differently and treating me differently." That feeling of being the different one is virtually universal among women in our Church, although the causes, the duration, and the seriousness of that alienation will differ with each individual.

Sometimes the feeling of being outside has a rational, identifiable cause; often it does not. Could a woman who grew up in a prominent Latter-day Saint family, married a man from another such family, reared outstanding children while amassing a whole list of professional and Church achievements, still feel like an outsider? Claudia L. Bushman, who meets this description, made these observations:

"One non-Mormon friend told me how much she wanted to be part of a group — to belong. When I replied that everybody felt that way, she said that I couldn't possibly understand, as I had the Mormons. Well, yes and no. It is true that we are all bound together. We have a structure with service built in and we would do anything for each other. At least someone would do it, out of duty, if not out of love. But for all that, we have plenty of tension and troubles. We are bound together by our mutual dislikes, our hurt feelings, and our insecurities just as surely as by love and service.

"People constantly complain of cliques and enclaves, of judgments and inadequacies in our little groups. They feel left out. They have part-member families, they don't live the Word of Wisdom, they are too shy to speak in church, they didn't go on missions, etc., etc. They think some wonderful hidden life is going on without them. I'd estimate that the majority of faithful Church members feel out of it for not measuring up to some idea or other while, on the other hand, some of those who feel most secure have little reason to be so, when measured by the same requirements. I often feel 'out of it' myself, and who is more in it than I?" ("A Celebration of Sisterhood," *Dialogue,* Summer 1987, p. 134.)

What a memorable sentence — "They think some wonderful hidden life is going on without them." A fact of human nature is that we tend to see others at their best and ourselves at our worst. We tend to idealize other women's lives in every respect. Something fulfilling and significant is happening, and we are not a part of it. We know what a struggle it was to get our own family to church on time, dressed and shining; we know how many impatient words were exchanged, how inadequate everyone felt, how a missing pair of socks was the pivotal issue in the morning's major crisis. But all we see of that other family is the array of beautifully dressed children climbing out of the van and arranging themselves in a neat row in the chapel. We give them the benefit of every doubt without stopping to consider what it probably took to get them there, what happens before or after this satisfying and impressive scene. How easy it is to exaggerate our own struggles and shortcomings and short-change ourselves on credit for our successes. We are quick to relegate ourselves to the outside.

Each chapter in this book focuses on women in a particular group: single women, women returning to activity, and so forth. To portray something about the women in these categories, each discussion begins with two case studies. In most instances these case studies are composite portraits, not stories of one individual woman but an amalgamation of bits and pieces of my own life, incidents from the

13

lives of women I know well, or just data from random observation. These glimpses draw no real conclusions. They simply describe a hypothetical sister and a little of her background, and the chapter does not seek to resolve these individual questions. But the case studies serve two purposes: first, for a reader in similar circumstances, they emphasize for her that she is not alone; and second, they may help other women to understand this particular woman, her concerns, disappointments, and hopes, and the events that brought her to her present situation.

Because separate chapters discuss separate groups, some readers may be tempted to turn only to the section that pertains to them. I ask you please to read all of the chapters. The point is not only to feel more comfortable with those differences that may belong to us personally, but to learn to understand others as well. We need an integrated sense of the variety of our sisterhood. We should go beyond tolerating our differences; we should rejoice in them, value them, grow because of them.

CHAPTER TWO

The Problem with the Patti Mold

When a woman feels like an outsider, just who is she comparing herself with? By what standard does she fail to be "in"? All of us can describe the ideal Latter-day Saint woman. In fact, we can list so many qualities that soon we start to laugh. No one could possibly have them all.

Two women living in Orem, Utah, Margaret B. Black and Midge W. Nielsen, wrote: "Many LDS women unconsciously compete with an idealized image of the already-perfect wife and mother who successfully incorporates all the demands of family, church, and society into her life. Although we have never met such a woman, we persist in believing she's out there somewhere. We can just imagine what she must accomplish in a day . . .

"Patti gets up very early and says her personal prayers. She zips her slim, vigorous body into her warmup suit and tiptoes outside to run her usual five miles (on Saturday she does ten). Returning home all aglow, she showers and dresses for the day in a tailored skirt and freshly starched and ironed blouse. She settles down for quiet meditation and scripture reading, before preparing the family breakfast. The morning's menu calls for whole wheat pancakes, home-made syrup, freshly squeezed orange juice, and powdered milk (the whole family loves it).

"With classical music wafting through the air, Patti awakens her husband and ten children. She spends a quiet moment with each and helps them plan a happy day. The children quickly dress in clothes that were laid out the night before. They cheerfully make their beds, clean their rooms, and do the individual chores assigned to them on the Family Work Wheel Chart. They assemble for breakfast the minute mother calls.

"After family prayer and scripture study, the children all practice their different musical instruments. Father leaves for work on a happy note. All too soon it is time for the children to leave for school. Having brushed (and flossed) their teeth, the children pick up coats, book bags, and lunches which were prepared the night before and arrive at school five minutes early.

"With things more quiet, Patti has story-time with her pre-schoolers and teaches them a cognitive reading skill. She feeds, bathes, and rocks the baby before putting him down for his morning nap. With baby sleeping peacefully and the three-year-old twins absorbed in creative play, Patti tackles the laundry and housework. In less than an hour, everything is in order. Thanks to wise scheduling and children who are trained to work, her house never really gets dirty.

"Proceeding to the kitchen, Patti sets out tonight's dinner—frozen veal parmigiana that she made in quantity from her home-grown tomatoes and peppers. She then mixes and kneads twelve loaves of bread. While the bread rises, Patti dips a batch of candles to supplement her food storage. As the bread bakes, she writes in her personal journal and dashes off a few quick letters: one to her Congressman and a couple of genealogy inquiries to distant cousins. Patti then prepares her mini-class lesson on organic gardening. She also inserts two pictures and a certificate in little Paul's scrapbook, noting with satisfaction that all the family albums are attractive and up-to-date. Checking the mail, Patti sees that their income tax refund has arrived — a result of having filed in January. It is earmarked for mission and college savings accounts. Although Patti's hardworking husband earns only a modest salary, her careful budgeting has kept the family debt-free.

"After lunch, Patti drops the children off at Grandma's for their weekly visit. Grandma enjoys babysitting and appreciates the warm loaf of bread. Making an extra call, Patti takes a second loaf to one of the sisters she is assigned to visit teach. A third loaf goes to the non-member neighbor on the corner.

"Patti arrives at the elementary school where she directs a special education program. A clinical psychologist, Patti finds this an excellent way to stay abreast of her field while raising her family. Before picking up her little ones, Patti finishes collecting for the charity fund drive.

"Home again, Patti settles the children down for their afternoon naps. She spends some quiet time catching up on her reading and filing. As she mists her luxuriant house plants, the school children come through the door. Patti listens attentively to each one as they tell her about their day. The children start right in on their homework, with mother supervising and encouraging them. When all school-work is done, Patti and the children enjoy working on one of their projects. Today they work on the quilt stretched on frames in a corner of the family room.

"Dinnertime and father arrive, and it is a special hour

for the whole family. They enjoy Patti's well-balanced, tasty meal, along with stimulating conversation. After dinner, father and the children pitch in to clean up so that mom can relax. She enjoys listening to the sounds of laughter and affection that come from the kitchen.

"With the teenaged children in charge at home, mother and father attend an evening session at the Temple. During the return trip, they sit close together as in courting days. 'Well, dear,' says Paul Perfect, 'did you have a good day?' Pat reflectively answers, 'Yes, I really did. But I feel I need more challenge in my life. I think I'll contact our Family Organization and volunteer to head up a reunion for August.' " (*Exponent II,* vol. 5, 1979, no. 3; used by permission.)

Most of us realize that when we laugh at Patti Perfect and the notion that such a woman really could exist, we are laughing partly at ourselves — at the way we want to believe, in fact, persist in believing that such a life is somehow possible. We give a crazy kind of credibility to a model that we all know is a joke!

It is intriguing that every time we laugh about Patti Perfect or some other impossibly perfect Mormon woman, our jokes portray a hauntingly uniform model. All of us come up with a fairly similar list of wonderful qualities: this Supersister can cook, sew, decorate, serve in virtually any church capacity, and she is always upbeat: she knows her mission in life, carries out that mission with energy, and never has to deal with self-doubt or depression. We all know what she's like. She's practically the same, no matter who is describing her.

Just one model? Just one way to live that is pleasing to our Father in Heaven? Of course we share some important qualities as Latter-day Saint women. In some respects we are the same: we seek to live righteously and obey the commandments, we support and value the family unit, we value the guidance offered by the principles, the scriptures, and the leaders that help us form our value system as Latter-day Saints. We don't claim the right, in the name of individuality, to be unkind, unchaste, or irresponsible. But to assume that all Latter-day Saint women are intended by their Creator to be exactly the same goes against what we know about our Father and the pleasure he takes in variety.

A trip to the zoo or aquarium, a botany course, or just simple observation will teach us an important truth: our Creator loves variety. It is almost as if he asked himself, "What are all the possible kinds of living creatures there could be? What are the possible ways they could look? What are all the possible colors and combinations of colors they could have in their various forms? What are all the possible ways of gathering food, of defending themselves, of reproducing, of moving through the air or water, of caring for young?" It may seem a little irreverent to use the word *game* in reference to the creation of our world and its creatures, but that is certainly what it seems to have been: a Divine Imagination stretching to create incredible and vastly different life forms, our Heavenly Creator taking delight in his amazing powers.

To mention only a tiny fraction of the mind-boggling facts of our natural world:

A kind of crab called a decorator crab cuts sea plants into pieces and pastes them on his shell to provide camouflage.

There are probably 1,000,000 species of beetles on the earth, 6,400 species of rodents, 300 species of lizards, and 1,800 species of frogs and toads.

The male bowerbird builds a fancy tent out of vegetation, even painting it with berry juice and other pigments, so he will have a beautiful place to perform his courtship dance.

Some penguins carry their unhatched eggs around on

the tops of their feet; after the chicks are born, they continue to ride around on the parents' feet.

A human has a total of 792 muscles; a caterpillar has 4,000; an elephant's trunk alone has 40,000 muscles.

The migratory ruby-throated hummingbird can fly five hundred miles without stopping.

The female gavial (or gharial), a reptile that looks something like a crocodile, lays her eggs under the sands of the riverbank. When the young are ready to hatch, they call to her from inside their shells to let her know it is time to remove the sand from above the clutch of eggs.

There has to be an easier way to do things! Do we need a million species of beetles? Do we need a creature with forty thousand muscles in its trunk? Isn't there a simpler way of engineering the hatching of the gavial babies?

But our Creator expressed himself through these and millions of other instances of natural variety. The conclusion is inescapable: our Father in Heaven delights in variety. He loves to see his creatures fulfill their lives and destinies, whether long or short, in ways that sometimes appear to us even fanciful and bizarre.

And within the species *homo sapiens,* each creation is unique. Surely it makes no sense, then, to think that a Father who loves variety, who cherishes differences and distinctions, would want all the women of his church and kingdom on this earth to be the same.

On the contrary. He intended us to differ one from another. Imagine a ward Relief Society made up entirely of Patti Perfects. Where is the delight, the humor? Where are the chances to progress? Where are the distinctive contributions made by the women who happen to work outside the home? Where is the spirit of sharing, where each sister looks for opportunities to enrich others' lives with talents she may have that they do not?

The Problem with the Patti Mold

It is safe to say, I believe, that as Latter-day Saints we do not have an "anchorite tradition" as part of our heritage. An anchorite is a hermit, someone who lives alone and gives up all worldly pleasures as part of a religious commitment. The closest we can come — and it's not very close at all — is the reports of long periods of time spent in prayer, such as Enos wrote: "I kneeled down before my Maker, and I cried unto him in mighty prayer and supplication for mine own soul; and all the day long did I cry unto him; yea, and when the night came I did still raise my voice high that it reached the heavens." (Enos 1:4.) As Latter-day Saints we do not idealize those who go off by themselves to establish a mystical relationship with their God. Our spiritual heroes and heroines tend to be those who work within a community to serve and lead. We are people who live and work together.

And our differences oblige us to live as a community, to be interdependent, to call upon and appreciate one another. Ward members combine their talents to make good things happen for other ward members. When a ward Relief Society plans a social, they usually want invitations, music, decorations, refreshments. It's not often that one sister has the talent and training to provide everything that's needed. But someone in the group is probably a fine singer or instrumentalist, someone else can plan and produce some outstanding invitations and decorations, and someone else will happily and capably take charge of the food. The Relief Society community orchestrates the abilities of its members to make the event happen, and all of us can take delight in an occasion we could never have brought into being on our own.

None of us by ourselves is Patti Perfect, but in any given ward or branch, when we work together, combining our talents and our virtues, we add up to Patti Perfect and then some. No one person has all talents. Our Father has chosen to give some talents to each individual while withholding or reserving other talents. It then becomes our great blessing to be able to supplement one another.

Sometimes we are too narrow in our definition of *talent.* Professor Elouise Bell of the English Department at Brigham Young University related this story about a young woman in one of her classes:

"Her name is gone now from my stockpile, but the face is not. She was a very mediocre student in a general lit class — worked hard, tried, came every day, but was just not gifted as a student of literature. One day she came up after class and politely asked if I would do her a favor. I expected a request for some after-class help, a chance for extra credit, a make-up on a low test. Instead, she explained that she was MIA [Mutual Improvement Association, now called Young Women] president out at the American Fork Training School [a facility for the mentally handicapped] and wondered if I would come out and tell stories to the group one Mutual night.

"I couldn't refuse, though I wanted to. I knew myself to be awkward, uncomfortable, useless in such settings. But next Mutual evening, I showed up. And there was my 'mediocre' student, surrounded by dozens of adoring admirers. She moved among those twisted bodies and stunted minds naturally, gracefully, and most of all, lovingly. She enjoyed being with them. She knew their names, their interests, their capacities. Her warmth made them glow. She was one with them. I have never forgotten that evening nor the lesson I was taught. Nor have I ever since been tempted to confuse mediocrity in the classroom with mediocrity of the soul." (*BYU Today,* Apr. 1984, p. 5.)

Each of us can, in some way, make another strong where she is weak. Each of us also must be willing to play the other role, accepting help from someone else to make up for our own weaknesses. Part of the pleasure of moving into a new ward is that in getting to know the sisters in Relief Society, we can observe how they form one whole. No one woman has all the strengths, but as they work together, there's not much that's missing. Even a small branch usually finds that their talents and resources, when combined, can make the things happen that need to happen and fill the needs that arise.

Especially in small branches, the members can often testify that the Lord sends them the person they need with the talents they need at the time they need them. In the fall of 1971 I arrived in Cambridge, England, to live and study for a year. I did not know one person in all of England, let alone Cambridge, and so I looked forward to Sunday when I could meet the members of the Cambridge Branch.

They were friendly and welcoming, but I was puzzled by the reactions of two people. One said, "Oh, so it's you." What did he mean? He didn't know me or expect me, any more than anyone else in the branch did. The other one said, "I'm happy to meet you, but you're late." Late??? What on earth did she mean? How could I be late, when no one in the branch knew of my existence before I walked in that morning?

But a young woman who saw my bewilderment explained what was going on: "Two weeks ago an American Air Force couple by the name of Jones was transferred from this area. Sister Jones had held five callings [not unusual in that small branch], and we were wondering who was going to arrive to replace her. The Lord usually sends someone our way when a need like this arises, and we're glad to have you here." Almost before I knew what had happened, I was sustained in four of the five callings Sister Jones had held. Even a small branch will usually find, I believe, that it is blessed with the assortment of talent it requires to carry on its essential work at any particular time.

Paul discusses this kind of interdependence when he compares the members of Christ's church to the members of the human body. In all the scriptures, no passage is more relevant to the issues addressed in this book than this one:

"For the body is not one member, but many.

"If the foot shall say, Because I am not the hand, I am not of the body; is it therefore not of the body?

"And if the ear shall say, Because I am not the eye, I am not of the body; is it therefore not of the body?

"If the whole body were an eye, where were the hearing? If the whole were hearing, where were the smelling?

"But now hath God set the members every one of them in the body, as it hath pleased him.

"And if they were all one member, where were the body?

"But now are they many members, yet but one body.

"And the eye cannot say unto the hand, I have no need of thee: nor again the head to the feet, I have no need of you." (1 Corinthians 12: 14–21.)

Implicit in this passage is an important message: it is not becoming or appropriate for the ear to complain that it is not an eye, nor for the foot to spend its energies worrying it would rather be a hand. As much as I would like to paint and draw, I will never be able to do so well, no matter how great my desire or how extensive my training. It seems my Creator chose to withhold those gifts. My job is to cultivate the talents I do have rather than to focus ungratefully on those I do not have. I can make other contributions for the well-being of the "body" of the Church. Just as the human body needs every part and organ, so the Church needs me and every other woman.

We can best fulfill our destiny by being ourselves. In his most famous poem, "The Love Song of J. Alfred Prufrock," T. S. Eliot allows us to listen to the thoughts of a pathetic figure who has wasted his life in a futile attempt to measure up to an image he feels others expect. In one of the saddest statements in the whole poem, J. Alfred Prufrock states, addressing himself,

There will be time, there will be time
To prepare a face to meet the faces that you meet.

For each new person or situation, Prufrock must don a new mask, a new face. Instead of cherishing his own gifts and cultivating a self based on his own personality, he channels his energies in different directions: attempting to be a false self for each new circumstance with "a hundred visions and revisions." He feels he must reaudition for each new set of circumstances. He has lived without a genuine identity, without spontaneity, without joy: "I have measured out my life with coffee spoons," he says. (In *Collected Poems, 1909– 1962*, New York: Harcourt, Brace and World, 1963, lines 26– 27, 33, 51.)

Several years ago, William G. Dyer, a faculty member the BYU School of Management, gave a forum address titled "On Becoming an Authentic, Congruent Person." An authentic, congruent person — the opposite of J. Alfred Prufrock — is someone with inner peace and a confident sense of self. An authentic, congruent person is able to achieve a consistent correspondence between inner values and outward behavior. I have never forgotten one story he shared with us in that talk:

"Some years ago I decided to try to respond more directly to my own warm and loving feelings when it was appropriate according to my values. I realized that when my four sons were younger, I had hugged and kissed them, but as they grew older, for some reason I stopped that most satisfying behavior. I discovered that I still felt like showing my affection, and reasoned that to be more congruent, I should act more directly. I decided to hug and kiss my sons and to share openly this affection, particularly when I left or returned from a trip. I've always been able to share affection with my daughter, but with my sons, as the scripture says, there was the 'fear of men.' I think my boys were a little uneasy at first at this revival of physical affection, but I also think that they liked this response from their father. I know that I enjoyed the reciprocal experience when a son would spontaneously come up behind me and grab me in a big bear hug.

"One day I was faced with an interesting situation. One of my sons offered to take me to the airport as I was leaving on a trip. He invited a young lady to drive with us. When we got to the airport I thought, 'Should I hug and kiss my son as I usually do, or would that embarrass him?' I then concluded that I had the right feelings. He also knew that I was a kissing father, and that was *his* problem. If he didn't like it, then he would have to be congruent and let me know. So I hugged and kissed my son as usual. There was no apparent embarrassment in him, and I think he would have been disappointed in me had I abandoned our usual practice. At that point, *not* hugging and kissing him would have been incongruent on my part" (*Choices: A Father's Counsel,* Salt Lake City: Deseret Book Co., 1980, pp. 106–7).

William Dyer knew his instincts were correct, and he knew he should act on them without letting the "fear of men" get in his way. How wonderful to be able to step forward and be ourselves, without seeking to meet false expectations or a uniform model!

"Ye are the salt of the earth," the Savior told his followers in Matthew 5:13. Developing this metaphor, the Christian writer C. S. Lewis suggests that we imagine a person who knows nothing about salt. "You give him a pinch to taste and he experiences a particular strong, sharp taste. You then tell him that in your country people use salt in all their cookery. Might he not reply 'In that case I suppose all your dishes taste exactly the same: because the taste of that stuff you have just given me is so strong that it will kill the taste of everything else.' But you and I know that the real effect of salt is exactly the opposite. So far from killing the taste of the egg and the tripe and the cabbage, it actually brings it out. They do not show their real taste till you have added the salt." In much the same way, each follower of Christ accepts his teachings and then goes forth to act upon those teachings in performing good works and serving as a light to the world in a way no one else can. As C. S. Lewis said about salt when it is added to vastly different foods: "It is something like that with Christ and us. The more we get what we now call 'ourselves' out of the way and let Him take us over, the more truly ourselves we become." (*Mere Christianity,* New York: Macmillan, 1970, pp. 173–74.)

Our Father in Heaven has created us with differences. He does not expect us to belittle or erase those differences. When a woman auditions for the Rockettes chorus line at Radio City Music Hall in New York City, her goal is to be exactly the same as the other women. Rockettes are supposed to be perfectly uniform, absolutely indistinguishable. The Church of Jesus Christ of Latter-day Saints is not the Rockettes! We do not seek to be the same! We seek to nourish our individual personhood. Our Creator made us different, and it is our privilege and blessing to preserve those differences, develop them in the most positive way we can, and offer them back to him in his service.

CHAPTER THREE

The Single Woman

Marital status is perhaps the greatest marker that divides "insiders" from "outsiders" among Latter-day Saint women. From all around comes the message that happiness means family, and family means a husband plus a wife plus their children. Latter-day Saint girls virtually always envision their future in terms of this happy, intact family. It's a little like Noah's ark: the world is supposed to be arranged two by two. A single woman may feel like the orphan sock left on top of the dryer in the hope that the mate will turn up someday.

First Case History

Charlene grew up in Centerville, Utah, near Salt Lake City. She and her best friend enrolled at Brigham Young University after they finished high school. Within a year and a half her friend was married, but Charlene has continued her studies as an English major. She loves her literature classes and consistently gets high grades. She thrives on the friends and opportunities at BYU. When she looks back at some of the journal entries she wrote as a naive, self-focused freshman, she realizes that her awareness, her spiritual sensitivity, and her self-confidence have grown immensely. Yet every time she returns to her parents' home for a vacation or a weekend stay, the people in her home ward greet her with the same question: "I just can't understand it, Charlene . . . why hasn't some nice young man snapped you up yet?"

And they are not the only ones who had assumed Charlene would be engaged or married by this time. Charlene had thought so, too. That is why she hasn't really made any plans for a career or graduate school. The skills she has acquired as an English major give her a broad competence that would be useful in many professions, but she realizes that employers are not exactly standing in line to offer her a wonderful job. Several of her professors have encouraged her to apply to graduate school. One of them suggested several universities on the east coast, but that would mean uprooting herself to face challenges and people she has not met before. Whenever she starts to think about applying to graduate schools on the other side of the country—or, for that matter, anyplace but BYU—self-doubt wins the day.

Charlene sees a few other young women "writing their own scripts," setting off with a real sense of adventure in pursuit of exciting educational or career plans, and she is disappointed not to find that courage within herself. The question is, what are her alternatives?

Is it possible that Kevin is supposed to be the answer? He is a good, kind-hearted young man, a returned missionary, and a sophomore at BYU, but he has not yet set any definite academic or career goals. He does not share Charlene's interest in literature or the fine arts. They enjoy being together, but when they are with friends Charlene can't help but feel embarrassed once in a while at Kevin's immaturity. She has noticed that Kevin laughs when no one else does, and then, when someone says something she thinks is delightful or funny, he is often the only one who does not laugh. He is tuned in to a different frequency.

Charlene is bothered by what happened one evening as they were driving home from a fireside. Another driver cut in front of them too closely, striking the right front of the car with quite a whack and sending them spinning to the side of the road. Fortunately, no one was hurt, but Kevin's immediate concern was for the damage to his car. Only after he had looked at the damage to his car and spoken briefly with the other driver did he think to see if Charlene was hurt or upset.

But Kevin is security. She is glad when he calls her for a date, and they almost always have a pleasant enough time together. Nevertheless, Charlene feels an immense sense of relief and freedom when midnight finally arrives and it is time for him to go home. She loves regaining her privacy, and she welcomes the chance just to forget about the whole issue of Kevin for the moment. It has occurred to her that if they were married, midnight would arrive and Kevin would already *be* home. How would she feel then? She doesn't like to dwell on it.

Kevin himself is certain they should get married. He says that the answer to his prayers about their marrying has been a positive yes. Her prayers have yielded no such definite answer. When she really thinks about being married to Kevin one year or ten years or forty years in the future, the foreshadowings of frustration and disappointment seem fairly conclusive. Yet she partially cancels those negative thoughts by saying to herself, "Any marriage is a leap of faith. You have to trust some things to work themselves out. We are very different from each other, but that just means we'll have to be tolerant and understanding, and isn't that how you grow?"

At the moments when Charlene is most honest with herself, she knows that the main attraction Kevin has for her is that marriage to him will mean she will not have to decide what to do with her life.

Second Case History

Barbara is a single woman who has a Ph.D. and a thriving practice as a clinical psychologist. Her specialty is teenagers; when a young person runs into problems with schoolwork, drugs, self-esteem, or the police, Barbara's long-established reputation means that she is likely to be called on to help out. She has a nonjudgmental attitude and a talent for creative approaches, and her clients usually leave her office feeling much better than when they came in. She cannot imagine any work that would give her more satisfaction.

Sometimes she opens a counseling session by saying to the teenager, "I realize that there are things you would rather be doing than sitting here talking to a middle-aged woman." The self-deprecating remark is intended to remove some of the tension and induce a smile, and it usually does, because Barbara at age forty-three is an attractive and young-looking woman. She enjoys being fashionable in dress, hair, and makeup, and she considers fashion one of the rewards of her professional success. She sometimes jokes that the most gratifying moment of her counseling career was the time when a fourteen-year-old girl asked her, in the middle of a counseling session, "Dr. Jones, where do you buy your clothes?"

The Church has always been an important part of her life. She does not, of course, seek to impose her values directly on her clients, but after all, the goal is to help the clients establish satisfying priorities and happy lives, and Barbara has always felt that the gospel, as her anchor for a happy life, gives her a valuable and deeply-ingrained personal point of reference.

She has served in Young Women and has been a Relief Society visiting teacher for many years. Currently she is Social Relations/Compassionate Service Leader in Relief Society. Attendance at her lessons runs very high, probably because the sisters are intrigued with insights and anecdotes from her professional experience.

Yet Barbara feels cut off in many ways from her ward. She has often asked herself about the source of this feeling: is she the one who is defining herself as an outsider, or is that actually the message she is getting from the ward members?

She knows there is no malicious intent in anyone's heart when the computer-addressed ward mailings come to "The Jones Family." She doesn't mind that she is usually not invited to elders quorum or high priests group parties. What bothers her more is that some people in the stake seem to assume that a single woman, no matter what her age and achievements, is not really an adult. One home teacher looked around at her spacious condominium and said, "One thing I could never figure out is why one person would need this much space." He seemed to think a single woman should continue to live in a student apartment. And for many years now, in Barbara's stake, a married couple has been called to be in charge of activities for the single people in Barbara's age bracket.

Occasionally a well-meaning relative or acquaintance will arrange to introduce her to an eligible single man. Obviously they feel she must be lonely. She isn't. The solitude of her condominium is welcome to her after a day of counseling, and she has many friends, both male and female.

She has often sensed that the bishop doesn't know quite what to do with her and the two other single, professional women in the ward. When he talks with any of these three, he appears uncomfortable. They seem so different from the women in his own family; how can he feel confident he knows their needs and wishes? He is always cordial and appreciative, and Barbara knows he recognizes the outstanding way she fulfills her calling, but she has the sense that if she were to go to him and say, "I've bought a new home, so I'll be moving to another ward," he would be secretly relieved.

In Meredith Willson's *The Music Man,* Mrs. Paroo, the mother of Marian the Librarian, asks her unmarried daughter:

When a woman's got a husband and you've got none,
Why should she take advice from you,
Even if you can quote Balzac and Shakespeare
And all them other high-fallutin' Greeks?

The message of this song is that if you are not married, nothing else about you — no status, no achievement, no amount of high character — can truly establish your credibility and acceptance. Many single women know that feeling all too well.

People with negative views about being single may turn up anyplace, including in the wards and stakes of the Church. We may encounter them as speakers, writers, teachers, administrators. To be sure, most of them are not saying, "Being single is really terrible." They are trying to be encouraging and positive. But consider this parallel:

My stepson, Wes, is a handsome boy. Everything about him is wonderfully good-looking, including his ears. But what if one day I began to reassure him about his ears, in a condescending way, over and over again? "Wes, you know, there's really nothing wrong at all with the way your ears look. Believe me, they're just fine." A few days later: "Wes, I know that sometimes when you look in the mirror you may start to worry about your ears, but I don't want you to give them another thought. They're perfectly all right; don't let anyone tell you otherwise." And again, sometime later: "Wes, you'll always remember, won't you, that there's no reason a person should ever be unhappy just because of his ears." What would happen in Wes's thinking if I were to say those things? My unspoken message is far stronger than my spoken one. Wes learns, once and for all, not only that his ears are funny-looking but also that I expect him to feel unhappy and embarrassed over his ears. That is exactly what I have *not* said — I told him not to be embarrassed, that his ears looked fine — but because I gave him so many condescending pats on the head with the supposed motive of reassuring him, I've helped him create a low self-image.

Here's the important point: all that would have been necessary for him not to worry about his ears would have been for me to say nothing at all. The more I said, "Don't worry, your ears are fine," the more I convinced him his ears weren't fine after all.

In my many years as a single Latter-day Saint woman, I have heard too many "Wes's ears" talks. One speaker at a stake conference said, "Now, you dear single people, I want you to know that the Lord is mindful of the special burdens you must bear. I want you to know that the Lord really does love you." Those are innocent statements, meant to be kind and supportive, but they imply some troubling untruths. What "special burdens"? Surely married people have "special burdens" too? Not in this speaker's mind. His "special burdens" phrase defines the world of the single Latter-day Saint as a bleak world of struggle and dissatisfaction. It then follows that this (of course unhappy) single person would have reason to doubt the Lord's love and would appreciate the speaker's assurance that he or she was not excluded.

President Gordon B. Hinckley has shown an impressive

awareness of the problem. He said to Latter-day Saint singles in a fireside satellite broadcast: "Somehow we have put a badge on a very important group in the Church. It reads 'Singles.' I wish we would not do that. . . . Because you do not happen to be married does not make you essentially different from others. . . .

"You are just as important as any others in the scheme of our Father in Heaven, and under His mercy no blessing to which you otherwise might be entitled will forever be withheld from you. . . .

" . . We do not pity you, for you do not want pity. You want opportunity and challenge and appreciation" (*Ensign*, June 1989, p. 72).

Unfortunately, not everyone is so wise. By the time a Latter-day Saint woman has passed the usual time for marriage and is still single, a whole host of remarks, interactions, and examples are likely to have taught her that she is expected to be unhappy. The emphasis in our Church upon marriage and family is so strong that it is difficult for many people—single or married—to believe that a life outside that pattern can be a happy one. Married life and single life are two different worlds, and here are the lists that supposedly describe the contrasts between these worlds:

Married life	Single life
Life at the center	Life at the fringe
Real life	A temporary condition, not real life itself
Something to preserve	Something to be changed as soon as possible
The real thing	Veneer or imitation
Normal life	An aberration
Progress	Paralysis

If a single woman (like Barbara in our second case history) dares to be happy in her life, the message from some ward members is, "Then you had better realize how unhappy you really are and start acting that way!" It is almost as if married people, having chosen to make the inevitable sacrifices that marriage requires, feel threatened when they see a single person who is as happy as they are—maybe even happier.

The fact is that no sociological study has ever shown an automatic correlation for women between marriage and happiness. So the message of this chapter is not the message conveyed so often by well-meaning people like the stake conference speaker I heard: "You single people must be patient and make the best of a bad situation."

Instead, the message of this chapter is this: single life has equal potential with married life to produce happiness, satisfaction, achievement, and spiritual progress. There is nothing inherent in single life that should automatically draw pity from self or others, or a feeling of injustice or unfairness, or low self-esteem. Too many Latter-day Saints accept a strange definition of what single life should be, a definition that requires single people to wait in the wings, looking toward the *future* for happiness, meaningful relationships, fulfillment, and credibility. This "life on hold" is a false world of our own making, created by people with good intentions, perhaps, but with limited understanding.

So single people don't need to be comforted. What they may need is a reminder that certain negative myths about being single—those cited in the "single life" list above, for example—are very much alive and that whenever such myths begin to influence our speaking, our actions, our planning, and our policies, it is essential to recognize them and avoid being limited by them.

Obviously, certain blessings that are highly prized—a

sustained, intimate, loving relationship with one man, the bearing of children—are not options for a Latter-day Saint woman as long as she is single. But she has other options to a degree that a married woman hardly ever has: choices regarding her own education, her career, the level of commitment to that career, and her geographical location. If a woman is throwing her heart into the education or career she loves, with friends and hobbies of her own choice, and still chooses to let the negative voices prevail, the ones saying "but surely as a single you can't really be happy," she should consider whether she is too susceptible to false opinion.

Sometimes the strongest messages of puzzlement and disappointment come from parents whose daughter remains single past the usual age for marriage. What can she answer when they ask her, "When are you ever going to find a man and settle down?" One young woman noted, "It got to the point where my parents were even asking me where they had gone wrong; they were blaming themselves for my being single. So I told them, 'You are wonderful parents, and the proof of that is that you brought me up to be self-reliant and happy. I love you, and I know you'll love me and support me whatever the future brings, whether I'm single or married.' "

All too often a single woman, particularly a younger one, will think, "If I achieve too much, I will price myself out of the market. I will be too intimidating." Here is the paradox: she probably dreams of her ideal mate as a man of wonderful breeding, education, and achievements. But in many cases she doesn't stop to think that unless she also is that calibre of person, their paths are not even likely to cross! The greater visibility and increased contacts that come with professional achievement may enhance her chances of meeting an eligible man of similar background.

Another woman may say, "But if I choose a path in my

education or career that requires a commitment of many years, what if an opportunity for marriage comes along and I have to drop everything?" I would answer, "Fine. So you have to alter your plans. What have you lost? You have grown; you have more individuality and experience to contribute to your marriage. And what does 'drop everything' mean? You will have decades of active life in front of you after your last child has left home. Many opportunities are likely to arise for you to benefit from, and ultimately continue, your training and experience." By contrast, if she sets aside the responsibility for her own planning and her own choices, she loses either way—in her happiness and self-esteem as a single woman, and in her contributions to her family and community as a married woman.

What would we think of a man who said, "One day I might be called as a mission president. If that happens, my profession would be interrupted. So I might as well just live from month to month, without any real professional commitment." That is strange reasoning, of course. First of all, he is wrong to let a future possibility drain all the vitality from his present dedication and achievement. And second, years of thumb-twiddling would be the poorest possible preparation to be a fine mission president. By waiting passively for the call, he will probably disqualify himself for it.

A study carried out in 1981 yielded some thought-provoking demographic information about single people in the Church. The study found that for every one hundred active single women over age thirty, there were only nineteen active men. In addition, the single women were more likely to have higher levels of education and employment. One report on this study concluded, "Clearly, marriage to an active male is demographically impossible for many active single females over 30. And even when there are available males, they may possess other personal characteristics that rule them out as potential mates. Marriage is not a universal solution to singleness if the only acceptable marital option is marriage to an active LDS partner." (Kristen L. Goodman and Tim B. Heaton, "LDS Church Members in the U. S. and Canada: A Demographic Profile," *AMCAP Journal,* vol. 12, no. 1, 1986, p. 89.)

If I had a daughter, I would advise her to set her educational and career goals as if she were going to live her entire life as a single woman. Then, if an appropriate opportunity for marriage should come along, she is that much farther ahead in her own growth and happiness and she has not made the error, in the meantime, of postponing her life on the assumption that someone will someday come along and make her happy. I would feel confident that her marriage would be happier because she had been a happy single woman. I have yet to see marriage, by itself, turn an unhappy person into a happy person. A really happy married person is almost always one who was or could have been happy as a single person.

Sometimes a young woman will obtain her education by acting from a very limited set of motives. She is the victim of what some have called "the mattress theory of education": education merely to give her something to fall back on! Of course it is important for her to be able to earn a living for herself, or for herself and her children, if no husband is present to provide that financial support. But that is only a default reason for education. She should seek the finest education that is within her grasp because she is a daughter of her Father in Heaven and when she returns to him, she wants to be able to say, "I have grown. I have made the most of the talents and gifts you have blessed me with. I have developed these gifts and used them to serve others." That is a far loftier, far more significant reason for education. "I am seeking an education in case the fates decree I must earn a living," as important a reason as it may be, is a pathetic, secondary motive by comparison.

Sometimes a single woman will seem to make a point of living a tentative, uncommitted life. She accepts a rootless, day-to-day routine, a makeshift and temporary existence that, according to her thinking, cannot become purposeful and real until she marries. Only a married person, so the myth goes, can lead a life of commitment and focus. Single people — particularly single women — are only camping, because they have to be ready to pull up stakes and make radical changes in their lives if "it" happens. The myth says that putting down roots not only causes inconvenience if single individuals marry but may actually endanger their chances of getting married or at least make those individuals seem less available. In any case, putting down roots, establishing a real life instead of camping, is (according to the myth) an inappropriate signal. It tells the world that the single person may have given up hope and not be gearing her entire life toward a hoped-for marriage.

In the newspaper one day was a letter to a psychologist-columnist from a single woman who complained that she was just not meeting any single men and did not know how to widen her prospects. The columnist answered: "Every year, you should move to a new city. Find a new job, a new apartment, and a new set of friends." On the surface, this advice seems to have something to recommend it: obviously, meeting eligible men was a high priority for this young woman, and the counselor's suggestions were intended to help her to meet more people. There is just one problem: that is not the way an adult lives. What about long-lasting relationships other than marriage? What about this young woman's career? What about the question of a true "home" (whether rented or bought) if she moves every year? A yearly relocation on the chance of finding a husband would make a shambles of the young woman's job prestige, financial security, and feelings of stability. Whether her chances of marriage would significantly increase with the frequent moves is a question I can't answer, but my guess is that if she were to stay in one place and give her energies to a career she loved, earning the respect of friends and associates, committing herself to Church and community, and developing herself as an individual, she would increase her ties, her visibility, and the quality of her own life. Unfortunately, the columnist, like so many other people, assumed that a single person just wouldn't want to think in such permanent, adult terms.

Two psychologists writing in a book called *The Challenge of Being Single* had some much more productive and helpful suggestions: "Despite the incontestable satisfactions to be found in a partner of our choice, there is plenty of evidence to suggest that an all-out search for such a person simply doesn't work. In fact, the search for the one-and-only may well be the most handicapping of all the mental 'programs' with which a single saddles himself. Many singles decide what they will do for a living, where they will work, where they will travel, and what they will do for recreation, driven by this search alone." (Marie Edwards and Eleanor Hoover, *The Challenge of Being Single,* Los Angeles: J. P. Tarcher, 1974, p. 22.)

Please don't misunderstand when I suggest that a single woman should be willing to put down roots, however. Sometimes what a single woman needs is to be willing to move. Each single woman should take a look at her career. Does it give her joy? Does it allow her to feel she has contributed in a significant way to the work of the world? Does she look forward to going to work each morning? If not, would additional schooling give her more meaningful work—a true career rather than just a job? Sometimes it's difficult to leave the security of a known environment. But I don't remember ever hearing a woman say that she regretted deciding to further her education, nor do I remember any woman who regretted relocating to pursue significant career advances.

It is frightening to think of moving to a place where we know no one. But we Latter-day Saints have an advantage — a network of friends who will help us make the adjustment to a new place. Many a Latter-day Saint (me included) has moved to a new location and has waited nervously and gratefully for the first Sunday to roll around, just so there will be some welcoming smiles.

I have talked to many BYU seniors who were reluctant to enroll in graduate school on the east coast or to accept a job offer in a strange city. My advice usually was, "Don't pass up this opportunity, but after you get there, be sure to suspend judgment for two weeks. At first you may well be saying to yourself, 'Why on earth did I ever do this? What was I thinking of?' But I can just about promise you that within two weeks you will be saying to yourself, 'I can't imagine life without these friends and these experiences.' "

I have known too many young women who should have been anxiously engaged in a good cause but who instead were preoccupied with anxiously causing a good engagement. An obsession with "finding the right one" can often paralyze a young woman in accomplishing other goals. My observation is that the best engagements are by-products, the result of truly being anxiously engaged in a good cause. The good cause is then sufficient reward in and of itself, whatever the social results may be. If a strong friendship or romance should happen as well, it is probably a far healthier, more legitimate pairing between two people with goals and interests in common than just "being on the prowl" would have yielded.

One psychologist has pointed out that it is a mistake to

equate marriage with maturity, because immature people often seek a spouse just as a way to avoid personal responsibility. "In contrast," he continues, "the singles who lead worthwhile lives have demonstrated their ability to live independent, mature existences. Mature, autonomous single people see life as a varied experience with many possibilities, contribute to others' welfare without making emotional demands, are self-reliant, and offer as much to a relationship as they take from it." (Rolland S. Parker, *Living Single Successfully,* New York: Franklin Watts, 1978, p. 178.)

One bishop told of a woman who came into his office, troubled and in tears, because the years were passing and she was still without a husband. "I never thought I would be this old and not be married," she told him. "I don't understand this. I have been preparing for marriage ever since I can remember." The bishop asked her to explain what she meant by "preparing" for marriage. It turned out that although she was a fine woman of high personal standards, "preparing" really meant mostly "waiting." She had denied herself opportunities for personal growth and new experiences because she assumed that someone else would make her happy. The bishop suggested that she undertake some new and significant goals on her own that would help her self-esteem and feelings of fulfillment.

In The Church of Jesus Christ of Latter-day Saints, we stress the importance of marriage as an eternal state, as the condition in which all truly righteous sons and daughters of our Father in Heaven will one day live. We are so accustomed to hearing this that we fail to realize that single people not only have equal opportunities for spiritual progress but also in some ways may actually find it easier to pursue certain spiritual goals than married people do. In 1 Corinthians 7:32–33, Paul writes: "He that is unmarried careth for the things that belong to the Lord, how he may please the Lord; but he that is married careth for the things that are of the world, how he may please his wife."

That is a somewhat surprising scripture, and as Latter-day Saints we do not automatically assume that a married person is a second-class spiritual citizen because he "careth for the things that are of the world." But most married women who have child-care responsibilities will tell you that they sometimes think back with longing to their single days when they simply had more autonomy, more jurisdiction over their own time, so that fasting, scripture study, and personal prayer were not so hard to schedule. Paul's statement should not give single people an excuse to flaunt a supposed spiritual superiority, but it is an interesting point to contemplate. With singles' greater autonomy and self-determination, is it possible that some spiritual opportunities available to single people are in fact more difficult for married people to find?

President Spencer W. Kimball often stressed that married people have no monopoly on the opportunity and responsibility for spiritual growth. At one point he said, in speaking to the women of the Church in September 1979, "Sometimes to be tested and proved requires that we be temporarily deprived—but righteous women and men will one day receive *all* that our Father has. It is not only worth waiting for—it is worth living for! Meanwhile, one does not need to be married or a mother in order to keep the first and second great commandments—to love God and our fellow-men—on which, Jesus said, hang all the law and all the prophets." (*My Beloved Sisters,* Salt Lake City: Deseret Book, 1979, p. 41.)

Our Father in Heaven did not send any of us to this earth to feel like half of anything. A true adult, whether she is married or single, establishes as happy a life as her opportunities allow, cultivates a close relationship with her Father in Heaven, and does not wait for another person to make her happy. All the important gifts of life are available to all of us: harmony, delight, increased skills and knowledge, close personal relationships, and spiritual progress. The Lord intends for each one of us to have a life of happiness, service, and satisfaction. But he does not have in mind identical timetables, identical life patterns.

CHAPTER FOUR

The Woman Who's Not
a "Lifer"

Does a lifelong, active member of the Church have a special claim on the "insider" designation?" Sometimes a newly baptized or newly activated woman may look with envy at a "lifer" — a woman who is the product of a strong Latter-day Saint family, perhaps several generations of such a family — and become very discouraged. The newcomer may say to herself, "I'll always feel like an outsider. No matter how strong my testimony is today, no matter how great my commitment, my past life will always keep me on the out-side." She envies the woman who has taken all the appro-priate steps (possibly a mission, certainly marriage and motherhood) according to the customary timetable. She has come late to a world in which others seem to feel far more comfortable than she does.

This woman is active in the Church, has a growing tes-timony, and desires to share Latter-day Saint values with others. The only difference between her and the lifers is that there was a time in her life when she did not accept and live the principles of the gospel. She has now made a new life for herself, and she rejoices in that life. But when she is around women who have always taken a Latter-day Saint life-style for granted, she still feels like a woman with a past.

First Case History

When Anita was growing up, *home* meant a place of physical shelter, a place to sleep and eat, rather than a place of emotional support. Her parents were divorced when Anita was just a year old, and she knew her father only vaguely. Sometimes on Christmas Eve he had come to the apartment with presents, but more than one Christmas had come and gone without a word from him. Even his physical appearance was a blur in her mind.

When Anita was twelve years old, her father died of kidney failure. Anita attended the funeral, along with her mother and her two brothers. Some of her father's friends from his car club attended, too. When they met Anita after the service, one of them said to her, "Oh yes, your father always carried a picture of you with him. He showed it to us many times. He was so proud of you." But not once had he conveyed these positive feelings to Anita in person.

As she looks back now on her teenage years, Anita feels that her mother probably did in fact love her. The problem was that she was almost always too exhausted or preoccupied to express that love. Rather than talk with Anita or involve her in household tasks, Anita's mother almost always preferred to withdraw to solitary television watching or resting. Her aspirations for Anita were minimal; some warnings about "you know better than to get yourself into trouble" were as far as her counsel went.

Anita was fairly regular in her high school attendance, but she was not a good student. Because she was very quiet, the teachers and counselors paid her little attention. Finally, out of boredom she tried cocaine. She did not become addicted, but more or less on an impulse she agreed to marry a twenty-eight-year-old man who dealt in drugs "only as a sideline." When she asked for her mother's signature on the document that allowed her to marry at sixteen, her mother responded, "Why not?" Anita never knew if her mother gave permission because she suspected that Anita was pregnant (she was not) or simply because she was relieved to get Anita out of the house and be rid of all responsibility for her.

Since that time, she and her mother have communicated only rarely. The marriage lasted only a few weeks. By then Anita was pregnant, and a solicitous social worker helped her through the pregnancy and birth. The social worker presented her with the options regarding the baby, and Anita knew that she would have to decide whether to give the baby up for adoption. After considerable soul-searching, Anita acknowledged that she could offer the baby virtually no security or opportunities whatever, and she gave permission for the adoption. It was the most difficult, heartbreaking decision of her life. Although she has never regretted it, she often thinks about the daughter she never even really saw.

Anita was now almost eighteen years old. The unfortunate marriage and pregnancy were behind her, but what did the future hold? She had no job skills, no niche to fit in. The social worker offered a suggestion: what about the United States Army?

Joining the army was the last thing Anita would have thought of, but she investigated the advantages of enlisting, including the chance to finish her high school diploma. She decided she had nothing to lose. Today, when someone asks her, "Would you recommend the army for young women?"

she answers, "In general, no. For the daughters of most of my friends today, the rough life of the army wouldn't represent upward mobility. But for me, it was exactly what I needed."

The series of small tasks and requirements, with daily and weekly successes as she made her way through basic training, gave her a feeling of achievement and self-esteem for the first time in her life. She began to look at the future in a different way, because she began to see herself as a person of worth who could contribute something to the world. She asked her friends to start calling her Anita instead of the series of tomboy nicknames she had always gone by.

The two nicest people she met in the army were a chaplain and one of the instructors who helped her toward her high school equivalency test. She found out both were Latter-day Saints. Because she was feeling proud of the way her life seemed at last to be coming together, she was open to any program or teachings that might help her to grow and mature. She attended a Latter-day Saint service on the base, and eight weeks later she was baptized.

Anita is now married and one of the stalwart members of her small ward in Texas. Though her husband is only partially active, she and her children consider the Church to be the core of their lives. Nevertheless, she feels a great gulf between herself and the other members. Sometimes she feels that her best course is to avoid all mention of her past—it *is past,* as she reminds herself several times each day. On the other hand, she sometimes thinks that if she were more open, she would feel less like a person with something to hide. What must people think of a ward member who never refers to her background, who never has relatives to visit, who seems to have sprung from nowhere? In any case, it is clear to her that the other women share experiences and assumptions that she will never be a part of. One day, for a lesson on gratitude, the Relief Society teacher had the Relief Society women sing two simple Primary songs. The others were laughing and joining in; Anita had never heard of either "I Have Two Little Hands" or "Thanks to Our Father." She wonders if she will ever truly feel a part of this group. She looks at the Relief Society president, a woman whom she particularly admires, and thinks, "They say it takes seven generations to make a lady. It probably takes about that many generations of Latter-day Saints to make a spiritual giant like her."

Second Case History

Evelyn decided many years ago, "If I can be polite to the people who visit me from the Church, and invite them in, and be friendly, then they can return the favor by not pressuring me to go to meetings." Evelyn's early activity in the Church had been sporadic, and when she went away to college she no longer received phone calls from a dutiful and concerned Young Women leader inviting her to meetings and special events. Accountable to no one but herself, she lost all connection with the Church. If anyone asked her about her religion, her answer was, "Well, I was *raised* a Mormon," with the intonation in her voice implying, "But I certainly don't consider myself one now."

She married a man who was not a member of the Church, and they moved several times in the years that followed. Each time she moved, her membership record somehow found its way to her new ward. Sooner or later there would be a phone call or a knock on the door, and someone would introduce himself as the home teacher or herself as the visiting teacher. In several instances, members of the bishopric or the Relief Society presidency had also come to visit. She appreciated their friendly intentions and knew that they were faithfully carrying out their assignments, so she was always hospitable.

Most of her home teachers and visiting teachers soon understood that Evelyn did not appreciate constant invitations to "come out to church." On three or four occasions when her husband was out of town for the week, she accepted, just for the sake of the company, her visiting teacher's invitation to homemaking meeting, but each time she regretted it. Her appearance at a church meeting caused what she considered a foolish flurry of fuss and anticipation, with everyone assuming she had resolved to become active. She winced when the visiting teacher kept saying, for weeks afterward, "We missed you at Relief Society!" They had not missed *her*, she felt; what they had missed, she thought, was the trophy of reactivating a lost sister, the triumph of adding to their attendance numbers.

Evelyn's world crashed in one day when her husband was diagnosed as having pancreatic cancer. His life expectancy was a matter of only a few weeks. Evelyn, always a practical woman, discussed with her husband what funeral arrangements he preferred. The outcome of these discussions was that Evelyn phoned for an appointment with the bishop. She was completely frank: "I am one of your inactives and I have made no contribution at all to the ward, even though I consider myself an 'ethnic Mormon,' if there is such a thing. My husband has no ties to any denomination, but he has decided that he wants a religious funeral service of some kind. He has appreciated the faithfulness of all my Mormon visitors, and he asked me to request a Mormon-style funeral service for him. I know you accept no money. I would make a contribution to the ward or whatever is appropriate. I don't want to impose." The bishop told her she was under no obligation and agreed to to anything he could to help.

The funeral was a dignified and appropriate tribute. Her husband knew and liked the hymn "How Great Thou Art," and Evelyn's visiting teacher and another woman sang it as a duet. Quite a few ward members came, and the nonmember friends who attended were impressed with the service.

Evelyn's situation changed entirely after her husband's death. She needed friends. She began attending church regularly and found that the prayers, hymns, and lessons were beautiful and comforting.

But as meaningful as she found her participation in the ward, she was sure she would never feel completely at home. So many other ward members had lived their entire lives at the center of church activity, proud of their achievements within the Latter-day Saint pattern, supported at every moment by relatives and lifelong friends. One Sunday, when a woman about Evelyn's age introduced a guest at Relief Society, "This is my daughter JoAnne, who is president of her ward Relief Society in Arizona. She is here with her husband and baby visiting me for a few days." Evelyn felt an envious longing for the same kind of firmly established, traditional Latter-day Saint security. Others had paid their dues all their lives; there was no way she could catch up.

To complicate matters, Evelyn's only son moved in with her after his divorce, and he was a chain smoker. The smell permeated everything in the house. No amount of bathing, shampooing, or laundering, Evelyn knew, could remove that smell from her hair, clothing, and skin when she went to church. Everyone continued to be kind and friendly, but Evelyn's feelings of self-consciousness and alienation increased as she continually wondered: How bad was the smell? Was her presence distasteful to other ward members?

The scriptures could not be more clear on the Lord's attitude toward the past sins and shortcomings of a person who has repented: he promises to forget them. He does not say he will discount them by a certain percentage, or that he will note them but not add them into the final account. He says that he will *forget* them. "Though your sins be as scarlet, they shall be as white as snow." (Isaiah 1:18.) "Behold, he who has repented of his sins, the same is forgiven, and I, the Lord, remember them no more." (D&C 58:42.)

When the Lord says he will forget, why do we think he does not mean what he says? Perhaps we need to create some images that will help us understand his promise:

The page on which our sins are written is shredded and then burned, leaving not even a pile of identifiable ashes.

The blackboard on which our sins were written is washed perfectly clean, leaving not even a trace of what was there before.

Someone at a computer keyboard pushes a "delete" button and the list of wrongs is gone, irrecoverably, from the data.

If the Lord forgets the sins of a repentant person, who are we to be more judgmental than he is? Many years ago a young woman I knew well had a baby out of wedlock. The baby was placed for adoption, the young woman resolved to begin a new life, and a year or so later she met a young man whom she married in the temple. I attended the reception, a lavish and joyful occasion, and as I watched the happy bride, I was shocked at my own thoughts: "She broke a major rule, and here she is celebrating a temple marriage! Is this right? Shouldn't she have to pay, somehow?"

I quickly realized that those thoughts were totally out of order. When I said to myself, "The Lord forgives her and forgets her past wrongs, but I choose not to," I was in essence saying, "The Lord forgives her and forgets her past wrongs, but I choose to outrank him. I am setting myself above the Lord because I presume I have the right not to forget."

A true understanding of the Atonement means not having to live with past mistakes. The Lord's forgiveness is real. The difficulty we have in truly dismissing forever our own past sins, and those of others, is a weakness in our testimony. If we continue to point the finger, to carry a grudge, to give a repentant person only tentative credibility, we are out of line with Latter-day Saint teachings concerning the extent to which blessings are restored to us after repentance: "It shall come to pass that every soul who forsaketh his sins and cometh unto me, and calleth on my name, and obeyeth my voice, and keepeth my commandments, shall see my face and know that I am." (D&C 93:1.)

What if our sins marked us forever? A famous verse from *The Rubaiyat of Omar Khayyam* shows the tragedy and despair of a world in which the past forever casts its shadow over the present:

> *The Moving Finger writes; and, having writ,*
> *Moves on: nor all your Piety nor Wit*
> *Shall lure it back to cancel half a Line,*
> *Nor all your Tears wash out a Word of it.*

(Translated by Edward Fitzgerald, in *British Literature 1800 to the Present,* ed. Hazelton Spencer et al., Lexington, Mass.: D. C. Heath and Co., 1963, p. 958.)

Imagine a world in which each wrong was there forever, in spite of our "Piety" and our "Tears." How different the Latter-day Saint view is! And what a foolish weakness on our part to say, "The Lord promises to forget our sins if we repent, but he doesn't really mean what he says." He does mean it.

What if you have forgiven yourself, and you know the Lord has also forgiven you, but the people around you do not accept the totality of that forgiveness? Sometimes there is little that can be done to open a small mind or to enlighten someone with a narrow and misguided attitude. Continued, consistent activity will add to your credibility and to the welcome you find in the ward; many a woman returning to activity has endured weeks or months when she felt awkward or embarrassed, as if she were being tested. But finally ward members have given her the benefit of the doubt. If some one ward member prefers to give a cold shoulder rather than warm acceptance, then that person has a weak spot in his or her testimony that only he or she can overcome.

The healing effects of a life of obedience and activity in the Church are great. Many years ago I had a calling as a counselor in the ward Young Women organization. One day, in casual conversation, the other counselor referred to the time she had been found "drunk in the elevator in the dorm at Brigham Young University."

The time she what??? I was stunned! This woman was the star young married of our ward, chosen for her calling because of the example she could set for the young women. I couldn't help but be curious: "So what happened? Didn't they throw you out?"

No, they hadn't thrown her out. She described how the bishop of her BYU ward, a wonderful man named Darrel Monson, had arranged for her to be allowed to remain at BYU in spite of her infraction. He had extracted a simple promise from her as the condition of remaining at school: she was to keep all the commandments *for a period of one month*.

That month of obedience was the turning point in her life. Bishop Monson, in his wisdom, knew that the happiness of a life of obedience is undeniable. He knew that as soon as she had a chance to compare the way she felt about herself and about the world during her "good month" with her earlier rebellious conduct, she would choose the path of obedience. Wickedness never was happiness, but righteousness *does* lead in the direction of happiness, and Bishop Monson was just arranging for her to find that out for herself.

I believe my friend decided to tell me this story from her past life for two reasons. First, we had known each other for quite a while, and it is natural for friends to be open. Second, she was already aware that I knew and admired Bishop Monson, and she knew I would be thrilled to hear what he had done for her. She did not recount the story very often; when she did choose to do so, she told it because she thought it could help someone realize the worth of repentance.

The question of "to tell or not to tell" is a touchy one. If the wrongdoings are truly cancelled by repentance, why mention them, ever? I once knew a man who could hardly let a testimony meeting pass without standing up to paint for the ward a vivid, detailed picture of the decadent life he had lived in New York before joining the Church. I could not escape the feeling that he actually enjoyed reliving those years. He also enjoyed the sensationalism and the dramatic effect of his own descriptions. Nominally he had repented, but in fact he reveled in the memory of sin. His repentance was incomplete.

And yet once in a while someone might feel prompted to revive the story of less-than-praiseworthy past happenings in order to help someone else. A woman I know spent virtually her entire married life as the wife of an alcoholic. She chose (rightly or wrongly) to keep his addiction a secret and to shield her husband from the consequences of his alcoholism. As the children became old enough to understand what was going on, they too became part of the protective facade.

Many years after this man's death, one of the daughters, now the wife of a bishop, phoned to ask her mother for permission to reveal the secret the family had kept for so many years. She had a particular reason: a ward member was going through similar problems, and she wanted to share her own understanding with her. After much discussion and prayer, the family decided that it was time to open the pages of that story that had been sealed so long and so carefully. Their motives were thoughtful and unselfish; they knew their experiences could lend strength to others and could give them far greater credibility, as people who had "been there," in their efforts to help others.

Leading up to the Savior's famous dictum that "the last shall be first, and the first last: for many are called, but few chosen" is the parable of the laborers in the vineyard. The owner of the house pays each laborer one penny, even those who had come "at the eleventh hour." The workers who had labored all day were resentful, as we might expect; but the owner said to them, "Take that thine is, and go thy way." (Matthew 20:1–16.) The scriptures constantly reassure the person who wishes to begin a new life that she does not need to feel like a lesser being. Those who come late to the vineyard receive no less. The angels rejoice over the one lost soul who returns. The shepherd leaves the sheep that are safe to search for the one that is lost. All rejoice; resentment has no place.

Imagine a ward made up entirely of people who had lived identically traditional lives. Imagine that there are no new converts, no move-ins with different backgrounds, no reactivated sisters. Although the people of this ward would have much in common and share many understandings, wouldn't it seem a rather dull group in some ways? The established patterns tend to make us set in our ways and smug in our assumptions, with the distinctive edges of our individuality becoming smoothed away. A new attendee with some new points of view — an investigator asking interesting and difficult questions, a new convert still struggling with the Word of Wisdom, a reactivated sister needing to be included in a group of long-established friends — will give the group an opportunity to reach out to another woman and extend to her some of the comfort and faith they enjoy.

The aim of the gospel is to change lives. As President Harold B. Lee once said to a faculty assembly at BYU, "The gospel is not a gospel of being. It is a gospel of becoming." All of us, if we are living as we should, are in a state of transition and self-improvement. We can support one another at every point in our journey along the gospel path, whether we are taking only the first tentative steps or whether we have diligently pursued the path for decades.

Christ's call, "Come unto me," was directed especially to people who had lost a sense of their own worthiness. They are the ones who have the most personal, most direct invitation to attend the meetings and discover the happiness offered by The Church of Jesus Christ of Latter-day Saints. The opportunity to make them welcome is one of the prime blessings of Church membership.

CHAPTER FIVE

Mothers Alone and Blended-Family Mothers

The job of rearing children alone is a daunting and serious responsibility. Whereas married mothers have someone who shares the burden of being the villain when it comes to discipline and the worry of being "the-buck-stops-here" person when it comes to decisions, the mother alone must rely on herself.

Most mothers rearing their children alone today are doing so because of divorce, and most divorcees count themselves in the "no-fault" or at least "not my fault" category. "Every step I took in my life was in accordance with the wishes of my Father in Heaven. I sincerely feel that," she may say. "I have always tried to be his prayerful and obedient daughter. And what was the result? I'm divorced." She is no less worthy than many other women who have the blessing and help of a caring husband; this apparent unfairness is difficult to accept. She feels cheated, because she was always told she would be blessed if she did what was right. And in The Church of Jesus Christ of Latter-day Saints, with its constant emphasis on priesthood responsibility and the role of the father as leader and patriarch in his family, the family without a husband and father runs the risk of feeling like second-class citizens.

In a somewhat different circumstance is the blended family. A blended family is fully staffed, so to speak, but it differs from the traditional family in that one or both parents is a stepparent to one or more of the children in the home. In a church that sees the family as an eternal unit, the blended family may feel like a patchwork anomaly.

First Case History

Beth, thirty-five years old, has been divorced for four years. She has two boys and a girl between the ages of eight and fourteen. That her marriage ended in divorce was the greatest disappointment of her life, but it also brought a sense of relief: it is easier to know that she and she alone is responsible for the family and its routine than to deal with her resentment toward an irresponsible husband who was present but did not share the adult responsibilities of the household.

When she first met Curt she had been attracted by his spontaneity and his free-spirit attitude toward the world. After she married him, however, it did not take her long to realize that words like *spontaneous* and *free spirit* were naive rationalizations. She had been blind to his selfishness and detachment. It was understandable—she was young when she met Curt, and she felt sure she was in love almost from the moment she met him—but as a married woman, and now as a divorcee, she had paid a high price.

During all those unhappy years of marriage, she had asked herself the same questions over and over: why did her husband get to choose to go off with his friends and play basketball, thereby choosing her to stay home? Why did he get to choose to be the one who could just flop into bed at night when he got sleepy, thereby choosing her to be the one to lock the doors and turn out the lights? Why were the responsibilities hers but the freedoms his? Even Curt's mother had acknowledged that marriage to him must have been difficult: "Well, at least you have one fewer child to worry about now, Beth," she had commented after the divorce.

Curt was an attractive, athletic, friendly person, and he had been very popular in the ward. Because they knew a very different Curt from the one she had to deal with at home, it was hard for some ward members to understand how Beth's patience had finally been exhausted—how, when it became more and more clear that divorce was the only alternative, even after she tried marriage counseling, she almost felt as if she had awakened from a bad dream.

Of course she now longs for someone to share such day-to-day responsibilities as home repairs and the children's discipline, especially as the children are growing older and need strong guidance. Yet she realizes that her own instincts, undivided and undiluted by Curt's random presence and contradictory responses, are probably worth more than two-parent input would have been if they had still been married.

Financially, Beth and her children are living almost at subsistence level. It is difficult for her not to feel guilty when she cannot buy her children everything their friends have. But at least she knows what money she can count on from her former husband's support checks and her new job as a medical receptionist; there is no Curt to do violence to the budget with the purchase of a new boat trailer or a twelve-hundred-dollar, radio-controlled, model plane.

Two years ago Curt remarried. The children visit their father and stepmother every other weekend, and it truly is a "visit": the children are guests, and it is always a celebration, with trips to Baskin-Robbins, the movies, the zoo or the mountains. It is party time. On the other hand, it is Beth's job to worry about orthodontics, school performance, homework, discipline, curfews, piano practice. When it comes to the difficult or confrontational aspects of parenting, she is the only one willing to risk the children's immediate displeasure.

The eight-year-old son asks almost every day, "Mommy, how many days until we get to see Daddy?" The two older children are more tactful than to betray how much they look forward to being with their father, but Beth can always sense their excitement as "Daddy's weekend" approaches.

Needless to say, the at-home-every-other-weekend routine causes many problems for the children's Church activity. What are the teachers and leaders in Primary and Young Men to do when they cannot work with Beth's children consistently toward an award or an achievement recognition, or when they cannot count on them to be present to rehearse or perform in a special program? Most of the time, though not always, the teachers have been very understanding.

A far greater problem in the children's attitude toward the Church is Curt's influence. He now considers his mission to have been a waste of time and money, and she knows he has communicated those cynical feelings to their fourteen-year-old son. Ward members make a point of referring to Curt in a positive way in front of the children, no doubt with the praiseworthy motive of helping the children maintain a good image of their father. But such comments only increase Beth's dilemma: how can she help the children love their father, and even respect him for his good qualities, while at the same time pointing out to them that many of the things he says and does are not only destructive and immature but sometimes out-and-out wrong according to gospel standards?

Beth is proud of the way she is able to manage her responsibilities. She has no shyness about asking her home teacher or another man in her ward to play the "father role" when it comes time for father-son campouts, and though she wishes she didn't have to ask, she finds that they are usually happy to respond once she gives them a little push in the right direction. She feels that the Lord has answered her prayers by sending her strength she did not know she had. It is understandable, therefore, that every time someone hints to her that she should, in effect, "solve her problems by finding another man as soon as possible," she feels that her achievements and efforts are being underrated and de-meaned.

Second Case History

Sandra, age forty-three, with three children of her own, is married to a man who has custody of his two daughters. As she often tells people, she considers herself "a big winner in the stepchild lottery," and she feels real affection toward the two stepdaughters. The two children of hers who are still at home get along quite well with their stepsisters. Sandra and her husband are each making a real effort to become more tolerant of the quirks and habits of the other's children and to be equal partners in the guidance and dis-cipline of all four children. They are proud of the new family unit they have formed.

Though Sandra's former husband has agreed to the can-cellation of temple sealings, he has made it clear that he will not at any time be willing to allow Sandra's husband to become the adoptive father of the three children. Everyone in the family tries to remember to smile each time they have to explain yet again why there are two surnames in one family.

But Sandra has a fantasy: if only her new family could move to the other side of the country, where no one knew them, and if her children, without anyone's permission, could just assume the new family name. The special distinction made in the ward list (cross-referenced between the two surnames) is clear and convenient, but it is a way of announcing a nontraditional family. Everyone seems to want to know how this came about. Some people have asked such questions as "Why did you get divorced? Why did your husband get divorced? Are you still sealed to your first husband? Why doesn't his former wife have custody of the girls?"

She reminds herself every day that she owes explanations to no one, and she tries to turn such questions aside without being too rude. Most people, thank goodness, have better judgment than to pry in this way, even though she realizes they are bound to be curious.

So why does she feel so accountable? Everything that signals their "difference" deeply disturbs her. Her husband's former wife maintains nominal activity in the ward where they live, and that awkward situation drove them to ask permission to attend another ward. They are the only family living outside the ward boundaries, and the ward boundaries and school boundaries put the children with two different sets of friends.

Sandra knows that the children worry about some deep, disturbing questions. So many of the lessons in Primary and in Young Men and Young Women relate to the joys of an eternal family, not the patched-together, confused arrangement that Sandra's family seems to be. Which family is the one that will "be together forever," as the song says, since both sets of children love both their parents and their stepparent? Which parents or stepparents — which grandparents, for that matter — will attend the graduations, speak at the missionary farewells, stand in the reception lines when the children get married?

Those of us who grew up in fairly sheltered environments and were not closely touched by divorce have sometimes been a long time in arriving at some kind of empathy and understanding for people in that situation. For many years I had heard sermons on "the evils of divorce." I, too, had read the articles in Church publications and elsewhere (I can imagine the effect of such articles on divorced women themselves) that sandwiched divorce among the most violent wrongs and deliberate maliciousness: "the great evils of our day are drugs, divorce, juvenile delinquency, alcoholism . . . " and so forth—as if someone goes out and commits a divorce just as she would a crime, or gives in to divorce just as she would an addiction. Nevertheless, the warnings had quite an effect. The thought of divorce sent a shiver down my spine. Better never to marry, I thought, than to be a divorced woman. (It did not occur to me then that a divorced woman with children she dearly loved would probably not wish to go back in time to decide not to marry and have children.)

Most Latter-day Saint women can remember very clearly the many Young Women lessons on temple marriage, the Standards Nights, the talks from bishops, parents, teachers. Those visions of the future were thrilling: the beloved wife of a noble priesthood bearer, each with an eternal commitment to the other, with children born in the covenant, in a bond that would never end. That was the life we wanted with all our hearts, that was the life we kept ourselves worthy for, that was the life we would have. Any thought of any sort of failure to meet this ideal might relate to one of the other girls, but that wonderful life was going to be ours.

No wonder the word *divorce* was a word of such horror to me for so many years! No wonder I felt such automatic pity and bafflement for anyone carrying the label "divorced woman"! How did I come to realize that divorce was not an event that necessarily involved wrongdoing on anyone's part? The turning point in my understanding came when I read a novel, *Middlemarch,* by George Eliot, first published in 1871. For the first time I got a close, convincing look at how two people who are seeking only what is best for themselves and others can make each other terribly unhappy in spite of their good intentions. In other words, I got an entirely new and enlightened perspective on divorce.

The story concerns Dorothea Brooke, a well-educated and intense young woman who has strong spiritual yearnings and a deep, meditative concern for sacred things. Even though most of the young women of her acquaintance are materialistic and superficial, Dorothea longs to serve the Lord and lead a saintly life.

Dorothea feels certain her prayers have been answered when she meets the Reverend Casaubon, a considerably older man who has never married because he has devoted his life to researching a multivolume compendium of biblical scholarship. She longs to serve as his assistant, to comfort his life and smooth his path so that he can finish this momentous and high-minded task. They decide to marry, and both feel confident that they will be happy together in a life of service and scholarship.

But the disillusionment is shattering. This is how George Eliot describes the despair that begins to overwhelm Dorothea almost immediately after the marriage:

"Her view of Mr. Casaubon and her wifely relation, now that she was married to him, was gradually changing with the secret motion of a watch-hand from what it had been in her maiden dream. How was it that in the weeks since her marriage, Dorothea had not distinctly observed but felt with a stifling depression, that large vistas and wide fresh air which she had dreamed of finding in her husband's mind were replaced by anterooms and winding passages which seem to lead nowhither?" (Boston: Houghton Mifflin, 1956, p. 145.)

Mr. Casaubon is equally unhappy. In the first place, he cannot understand what Dorothea could possibly desire that she does not have as his wife, and in the second place, he knows deep within himself that someone is gradually, inevitably, coming to know the truth about his "great work in progress," the momentous *Key to All Mythologies,* although the prospect of this forthcoming work of scholarship has sustained his reputation for decades, he does not really have the intellect to produce such a work. He has collected scraps and pieces, but they amount to nothing. There will never actually be a *Key to All Mythologies.* The marriage is a tragic disappointment.

I learned some important things from this novel. Both Dorothea and Reverend Casaubon were good people who felt there was a strong spiritual basis for their marriage. Dorothea was naive and Reverend Casaubon deluded himself, but neither deserved harsh blame. They shared equal disappointment over the failure of the marriage; both of them were basically sound, upright people whose actions did not deserve this kind of punishment.

I needed to read about this couple. I needed to balance Dorothea Brooke and the Reverend Casaubon with the many sermons I had heard stating that divorce is the result of sin, the outcome of broken commandments. Both points of view can be true, of course; nothing in the world varies more widely than the circumstances behind divorce. No two divorces are alike. But because I read *Middlemarch,* and because over the course of years I became more aware of differing circumstances as various close friends and relatives faced divorce, I became much more accepting.

I am particularly grateful for this broadened understanding because I was then prepared to apppreciate the man whom I eventually married. If I had met him ten or fifteen years earlier, my reflex reaction would have been, "Oh, no! I would never want to date a divorced man!" I would have passed right by a great and wonderful blessing. Divorce may signal serious personal deficiencies and wrongdoing, but this was one of the many times when it does not.

We are so accustomed to thinking of a one-parent family as a "broken home," as incomplete, that it can come as something of a surprise to realize that some broken homes are now far more whole than they were before the divorce. Some years ago a friend's husband decided after nineteen years of marriage that he had had enough of marriage, of family responsibilities, and of the Church, and so he left. Their bishop was aware of what was occurring. When her husband filed the papers for divorce, the bishop asked her to come to his office the following Sunday. She thought he was going to just check with her to make sure she was getting along all right and to offer some words of cheer. Instead, he called her to be the ward Relief Society president.

She was more than a little surprised. She asked him, "Isn't your timing a little unusual?" He answered, "On the contrary. I can extend this call to you now that the impediment is gone."

What insight! The bishop had perceived that after the divorce, the spiritual level of the home would be higher, greater peace would prevail, and my friend would be in a much better position to accept this demanding calling.

As Latter-day Saints, we cherish our picture of the traditional family pattern. But we should not let our ideal keep us from acknowledging and appreciating the many thriving, praiseworthy families that have another pattern. When a divorce occurs, it can be so devastating that the woman's first reaction is, "I can't go on." But then from inside her comes another voice asking, "So what exactly do you plan to do instead?" She knows that going on is her only choice, for her own sake and that of her children. Throughout the Church are families establishing their own identity even though no husband and father is present. They deserve our admiration.

Even a woman who does not go through a divorce herself may find that her life is strongly affected by someone else's divorce. The fact that my husband was previously married accounts for our blended family, because his teenaged son lives with us and his twelve-year-old son spends quite a bit of time with us. My two sisters are also married to men who have children by previous marriages. So, after my parents had lived for many decades without being closely touched by divorce, they now have three sets of stepgrandchildren. The realities of our modern world place many people in positions they thought they would never be in, especially with regard to their family arrangements.

Divorced women may often feel alone among the more traditional families in a typical ward, but they need not feel alone statistically as divorced women in the Church. A 1981 demographic study of Latter-day Saints in North America shows that although only 7 percent of adult Church members reported themselves as separated or divorced at the time of the study, fully one-third of them can expect to be divorced at some point by the time they are sixty years old, according to present trends. (See Kristen L. Goodman and Tim B. Heaton, "LDS Church Members in the U. S. and Canada: A Demographic Profile," *AMCAP Journal,* vol. 12, no. 1, 1986, p. 93.)

People all over the world are being called upon to form and help manage new family units, with new combinations of relationships and steprelationships. We do the best we can. Since genetics can sometimes play welcome tricks, I like to think that people can't necessarily tell by just looking at us that Wes and Eliott are not my sons, though there are bound to be a few, I suppose, who note how tall and good-looking the boys are and say to themselves, "She couldn't possibly be their mother!" I think it's usually when others hear the boys call me "Karen" that they know ours is not a traditional family.

When people refer to "your son," do I bother to set them straight? It depends. I don't want to convey incorrect information, so if the misunderstanding is liable to recur with the same person or have consequences later on, and it's important to be accurate, I just smile and say, "stepson, actually." Otherwise, if it's a transitory situation, I just let it go. The grim connotations of the word *stepmother* are all too well known. I don't tell Wes he has to stay home from the ball, and I don't send him out into the forest to get lost, and I don't feed him poison apples. So I would just as soon he let random references to his "mother" pass without comment, and usually he does.

Many books on stepfamilies are available, and families can also join stepparent support groups. In the books and in the discussion groups, certain "points to remember" for stepparents are emphasized again and again. Here is a summary of a few of the most important:

1. Do not expect to feel the same automatic feelings of love and acceptance toward your stepchildren as you do toward your own children. These feelings may come only gradually, or they may in fact never be as strong.

2. It is natural to feel resentment when your stepchildren take for granted all the things you do for them — your time, your effort, your concern. It's often said that mothers expect no thanks but stepmothers do. Mothers would like thanks too, of course, but they are perhaps able to accept their taken-for-granted role better, whereas the woman making personal sacrifices for the sake of her husband's children tends to feel hurt when her contributions are not recognized.

3. It is natural to feel resentment, also, when your husband appears to be putting his children's welfare ahead of yours. It may be that he also puts their welfare ahead of his own. In any case, that is a point to be talked through very carefully.

4. If the "other family" does not subscribe to wholesome values, weeks and months of hard, productive work can be undone in one short stay with the other natural parent. There may be little you can do about it except to continue to do what you know is right and try to rebuild.

5. Especially in the case of older stepchildren, no amount of love and effort may be sufficient to undo damage that has been done in past years.

6. Some young people may be problematical young people, period. Genetics may overpower anything that your training, example, threats, or encouragement can accomplish.

7. The two adults, parent and stepparent, *must* present a united front. It may be necessary even before the wedding for the two adults to spend considerable time writing down expectations for the children's behavior and discipline.

8. The stepparent should expect to be involved only gradually in the major disciplining of the stepchild. You might not be assuming the full role as a disciplinary parent for two years or even more.

9. In order to keep interactions between you and your stepchild as pleasant as possible, try to arrange as frequently as you can for some neutral source to be the "reminder" or "enforcer." For example, write down chores on a calendar so that you do not have to be the one to mention that today is the child's day to do the dinner dishes, and so forth.

10. Whenever possible, choose words without negative connotations. "When our marriage ended" is better than something more negative ("When our marriage broke up,"

or "When my husband left me"). Avoid "visit" when you refer to children going to the home of a parent; "stay with" is better, even when it is only for a few hours. Say "the children's father" rather than "my ex." Use the word "family" freely, without such footnotes as "but I'm divorced"; you and your children are entitled to be called a family! When someone asks, "Do you have a family?" just say yes. You do not need to add, "I'm a single mother."

This list of suggestions may seem to assume a negative, problem-ridden blended family household. (In fact, it might be enough to frighten someone away from a marriage that means not only a husband but some new, ready-made children as well!) Of course not all stepfamily situations are grim. But when problems arise, it helps to know that your family is not the only one that doesn't seem to be acting like the Brady Bunch. Only on television do six charming children, with nothing but pleasant words on their lips, come together into one delightful family, thereafter encountering no problem that can't be solved in thirty amusing minutes.

Mothers who tend to see their child's (or stepchild's) poor behavior and lack of achievement as an embarrassing reflection on themselves would do well to remember that most people have paid their dues, in some form, where child-rearing is concerned. Teachers, ward members, and other adults are likely to be far more tolerant than we give them credit for. They've known and observed plenty of young people, and yours is unlikely to be the worst. They probably realize that a young person, especially a teenager, is an individual with free agency, not an automatic gauge of the care and guidance he or she receives at home. Misbehaving children, then, as stressful a problem as they pose, should not cause a gulf of embarrassment to distance a mother or stepmother from other women in the ward. The mother of a problem child may be performing more heroically and effectively than anyone imagines.

A particular situation in a nontraditional family may call for some frank words with a church leader or teacher or ward member. The teacher may not understand that the every-other-weekend absence is actually stipulated by court order; it is not a matter of the child's preference or the mother's preference. A ward member who idealizes the children's father when the father is actually undermining their testimony and loyalty to the Church may need to be quietly informed of a few facts. A ward member who is too nosy about personal family matters may just need to be told, with a smile, "I [we] prefer not to discuss that." If the question concerns another person, just change the response slightly: "He [she] prefers not to discuss that."

A nontraditional family living outside the ward boundaries or dealing with other awkward fallout of divorce or remarriage may have to call upon every bit of patience and tact they possess. Sometimes a bishop or other leader may make it more difficult for a nontraditional family to work out an effective pattern for their lives. But leaders can be educated, new leaders can be called, and many courageous and persistent families throughout the Church have found their niche. For a woman rearing her family without a husband, the friendships and resources offered by the young people and adults in their congregation can make the difference between a feeling of uncertainty and isolation and a feeling of support and encouragement. For the mother of a blended family, the values of the Church provide a core around which the goals and activities of the newly formed family can be structured.

CHAPTER SIX

The Woman Who Is "Single at Church"

We've discussed women who are single. What about the woman who is married but who is, as one described it, "single at church?" When it comes to activity in the Church, her husband is the invisible man. In fact sometimes the other ward members don't even know what he looks like. In her wish to attend meetings and fulfill a calling, this woman may or may not have her husband's support. He may occasionally attend a meeting himself. Some husbands who are not Latter-day Saints or who are less active enjoy themselves at ward social and sports events, but many do not.

First Case History

Because her mother was a Latter-day Saint and her father was not, Elaine did not find it particularly frightening to contemplate marriage to a man who was not a Latter-day Saint. In fact, she had a lot of approval from family and friends when she announced that she and Frank were engaged. She had met him when they both were seniors at the University of Delaware. She and her family were impressed with everything about him; he had a self-assurance and a generous nature that comes with a commitment to a strong set of values. She knew that the ideal marriage would be to someone who was also a Latter-day Saint, but she was grateful that she and Frank were compatible in so many other ways. Her mother said to her, "Elaine, you've found a jewel."

After Frank finished his graduate program in accountancy, they bought a home in Connecticut. It was a wonderful place to rear their two children. The family settled into basically the same pattern that Elaine had known growing up: Frank acknowledged that Elaine's church and its program provided a vital center for Elaine's life and a strong set of values and principles for their children, and so even though he did not seriously contemplate being baptized a Mormon himself, he was happy to support his wife and children in their affiliation with the Church.

One day Frank phoned Elaine to say that he had just met with his boss, who had asked him if he would consider a transfer to Salt Lake City! It meant a promotion, and Elaine and Frank decided to go ahead with the move. Frank told his boss, "Since my wife and children are Mormons, they'll probably feel right at home there." And in fact, Elaine had always been curious about what it would be like to have thousands of other Saints as neighbors.

But their experience with the ward in Salt Lake was entirely different from what it had been in Connecticut. Elaine felt a real gulf between herself and the other women in the ward. In Connecticut Elaine had served for several years as Young Women president, but she feels that she will never be called to serve in the Young Women organization in Salt Lake because her marriage to a man who is not a

Latter-day Saint seems to make her a poor example to the young women of the ward.

When it comes time for an outing with the Scouts or a priesthood preparation program, the officers and teachers in the ward don't seem to know whether to treat Elaine's son as if he were fatherless or whether to assume Frank will be involved in some way. She understands that awkward confusion, but she feels that at the root of it is their perhaps unconscious belief that a man can be a good father only if he is a priesthood holder. Elaine gets angry at that idea, because she is convinced that there is no more involved, caring, or creative father in the entire ward than Frank.

Frank always attends church when the children are participating on the program, and he usually accompanies Elaine to ward dinners or other purely social events. To Elaine's great embarrassment, someone will frequently make the obligatory comments: "You have a great family there, Frank. Don't you want them with you forever? You're pretty stubborn, you know."

One day Elaine's visiting teacher seemed nervous. After a few minutes, the visiting teacher squared her shoulders — obviously there was something she felt she had to say, and finally she blurted out: "Elaine, why don't you just give your husband an ultimatum? Can't you tell him that either he joins the Church before another year goes by, or your marriage is over?"

Elaine was too astonished to be angry. How could this woman assume that the happiness and commitment that Elaine and Frank had achieved in their marriage was something to be used as a bargaining chip? Did she believe that no marriage other than a temple marriage could be a happy one? Obviously the visiting teacher assumed that the marriage she and Frank had built with such devotion over many years was something not worth preserving.

Second Case History

Marta and her husband Cliff often laughed about the "Yummy" label one of their friends had given them — "Young Upwardly Mobile Mormons." Though they were by no means wealthy, they were both professional people, and they enjoyed the things that they were able to afford through their two incomes. When their first child was born, Marta cut her accounting practice back to half time, and she enjoyed being a mother as well as a professional. They were one of the most visible families in their ward; in fact, the bishop had said to them at one point, "The young marrieds in our ward look to you as an example of what they're after."

So it came as quite a surprise to the bishop when, after Cliff had missed his Sunday meetings for several weeks, he asked for an appointment with the bishop to request that his name be removed from the records of the Church. That evening, Cliff called a few of their closest friends in the ward to let them know what had happened.

Marta was not surprised. She had known for quite a while that something was coming. But over and over again, ward members asked her, "What happened? Why did Cliff decide to do this?" Marta really didn't know how to answer questions about Cliff's motives. On many occasions she and Cliff had talked about his feelings late into the night. She had tried to understand. She and Cliff had subscribed for many years to two or three periodicals aimed at a liberal Latter-day Saint readership, but so did most of their friends. They enjoyed reading and discussing the articles, and often when they got together with LDS friends they had known since college days they discussed some of the issues. Was that the problem? Had Cliff "intellectualized himself" out of the Church by reading and pondering these out-of-the-mainstream materials? That was far too easy an answer. She and many of their friends had also read about and dealt with the same issues, and they had not lost their testimonies.

Marta was inclined to see Cliff's upbringing as the more direct cause of his dissatisfaction with the Church. Cliff was born in the Church, the son of an authoritarian father who gave his children very little freedom of choice. In Marta's mind, after Cliff's overbossed childhood, he had perhaps reached something of a midlife crisis triggered by the question of authority. Cliff had suddenly realized that he had never known a time when he was not following the script someone else had written for him. He had not even rebelled as a teenager. Now, as a thirty-nine-year-old man, Cliff could feel like an autonomous, free person only by rejecting the authority of the Church."

Cliff knew that his decision, which he felt to be honest and inevitable, jeopardized their marriage. He had said frankly to Marta, "You will have to decide whether your desire to be married to a Latter-day Saint husband is greater than your desire to be married to me."

Marta considered the possibility of divorce only briefly. She wanted to stay married to Cliff, and he wanted to stay married to her. He promised that he would not stand in the way of Church activity for her and the children. He made it clear, however, that he himself would not have anything to do with any event or program sponsored by the Church. He wanted, in his words, "a clean and complete break." The problem, especially as the children grow older, is that so many of their social and sports activities, as well as their Sunday meetings, center around the Church. By missing out on those activities, Cliff is missing out on a big part of his children's lives. Marta hopes the children will continue to find enough happiness and meaning in their Church activities to remain loyal in spite of Cliff's example.

Now that four years have passed since Cliff's decision,

Marta takes for granted her role as the only Latter-day Saint adult in the family. Once the initial shock wore off, the members of the ward where they had lived for fourteen years seemed to accept what had happened. Most ward members understand that she does not like to be asked such questions as "Is he coming around yet? Does he ever talk about coming back? Has he joined another church?" Their inquiries are usually limited to "How's Cliff these days?" and her answers are always brief. Cliff prefers not to socialize with couples from the ward, although they have maintained their friendships with a few college-friend couples who Cliff felt would understand and respect his decision and not press him to justify what he had done.

A few people in the ward don't know Cliff at all. A little Primary friend asked one of Marta's children one day, "Who was that man your mother was with at the mall?" "That was my father," the little girl explained. The Primary friend was surprised to learn that Marta's daughter had a father.

Marta and Cliff have what Marta wryly calls "an armed neutrality pact" in their marriage. Cliff's decision is firm, and the issue of his attitude toward the Church is off-limits for discussion. They are actually getting along better than Marta had thought they would: their strong marriage continues to be strong. Though his decision to leave the Church has caused her much unhappiness, Marta is sure she did the right thing by not sacrificing her marriage over the issue of Cliff's Church membership.

Marta feels especially sad, however, when someone else from the ward must step in and do what most of the fathers do for their children—the baptisms, the ordinations, the accompanying of her son to the ward-sponsored father-and-son campouts. She feels no less loved and accepted in her ward than she did before, but makeshift arrangements for these events are a constant reminder that her family, as far as activity in the Church is concerned, is incomplete. When she sees a father blessing a baby, when she sees an entire family sitting together in sacrament meeting, when she hears a lesson on the blessings of the temple, the sadness is always there.

One brief piece of wisdom valuable for anyone, male or female, married or unmarried, that might be especially useful to the woman whose husband is not a Latter-day Saint or is less active, is as follows: "Don't wait for someone else to make you happy." One friend of mine remarked, "I love Paul, but sitting around waiting for him to be baptized would be a drag."

Most women whose husbands are not Latter-day Saints report that nagging, needling, and bargaining are not very effective means of interesting their husbands in the Church. In fact, they find that if they refer constantly to their wish to have him attend a meeting, for instance, they build up such resentment that they lose hope of attaining their goal. One woman said that her aunt, also the wife of a man who was not a Latter-day Saint, gave her this advice: "Be an example of what the Church can produce, not an example of how persistent we can be in our missionary zeal."

Though it is inevitable that an active Latter-day Saint woman without an active Latter-day Saint husband will wish she could find some way to turn him into a happy, believing member of the Church, it may help her to realize that 21 percent of households with at least one adult Latter-day Saint consist of a Latter-day Saint whose spouse is not a Latter-day Saint. Of the households where both husband and wife are members (47 percent of the total) some proportion (these statistics were not given) consists of one active Church member and one less active. (The other 32 percent of the total households are single adult households.) So the woman who is "single at church" may not be as alone as she thinks she is.

One woman remembers the burden she carried as the child of a father who was not a Latter-day Saint. "Insofar as certain people in my ward made me feel my father was inferior, I just had to disconnect from them," she states. "Now I'm the one married to the non–Latter-day Saint husband, and on one of the rare occasions when my husband attended church, the woman speaking in sacrament meeting stressed the blessings of temple marriage. That was all right, but then she went on to refer to marriage to someone not a Latter-day Saint as a 'horrible compromise.' Well, my 'horrible compromise' was sitting right next to me, and it was a long time before he attended another meeting."

In an effort to help other ward members understand her situation, one wife of a less-active husband made two decisions when she moved into a new ward. The first decision was that on Sunday when she was asked to stand and introduce herself, she would say something like "My name is _____, and we have just moved here from _____. My husband is a wonderful man, but he has chosen not to be active at this time. I look forward to getting to know all of you better." The second decision was that every time she mentioned her husband's lack of Church activity she would, in the same sentence, refer to one or another of his good qualities. It was important to her that the ward know about her situation as the wife of a less-active Church member. It was also important to her that other ward members realize that this man was someone she loved and someone they would enjoy meeting.

Many women who are "single at church" find that some of the most troubling problems of all relate to their children. Other children may be cruel, consciously or unconsciously. If a woman whose husband is not a Latter-day Saint is a

Primary teacher and invites the class to her home, the children's shock when they spy a coffee can may be entirely out of proportion to that discovery.

Because a child cannot be baptized into the Church without the permission of the father, his or her baptism may be delayed beyond the age of eight—sometimes until age eighteen, when the young person may choose to be baptized without permission. Thus the rest of the Primary class may be celebrating their baptisms one by one, while the child whose father is not a Latter-day Saint must wait on the sidelines. Even the most sensitive Primary teacher will have a difficult time helping this child to feel part of the group.

One woman commented, "A few of the adults at Church seem to make the children responsible for the fact that one of their parents is not a member. I don't know why. It may just be ignorance, or it may be that they are carrying around a fantasy of the 'innocent little missionary' who is able to touch the parent's heart by rushing in where no one else dares venture. But I wish they would not urge my son to invite his father to church. That's not their role, that's not my son's role, and it only causes friction and disappointment. And one day a teacher told my son's class that only the members of our church were really on Heavenly Father's side. So where does that leave his father? You can imagine how that made him feel."

How does she handle her little son's worry over whether their family will be together in the next life? "I tell him that the ordinances are true and correct, but Heavenly Father considers a lot of things, including worthiness. I think that's the best way for us to deal with these worries."

How can ward members be helpful to a woman whose husband is not visible on the Church scene? Different families have different blanks to be filled in. One very important thing to remember is that in some contexts—purely social occasions or occasions involving his children in an important way—a man may choose to be visible after all. Once in a while a person who is not a Latter-day Saint will lead a life of virtually total activity, minus the baptismal ordinance. Many people can tell affectionate stories of Scoutmasters and other youth leaders who were not Latter-day Saints who influenced them for good in past years.

The ward, then, should complement his commitment to the extent necessary. Substitute fathers for the children's activities and ordinances may be needed often or almost not at all. In the case of a husband who is a Latter-day Saint but is less active, if his priesthood has not been formally removed, he is eligible to perform all the ordinances— baptism, blessing, priesthood ordination—to which his priesthood office entitles him, with the consent of the bishop.

Ward members are sometimes so anxious to welcome and impress a nonmember spouse that their enthusiasm may backfire. One woman was married to a quiet and re- served man who was not a Latter-day Saint. The first time he came to a ward social event—it was a Christmas dinner— her husband was put off by the repeated hearty hand pump- ing and loud welcomes from people he had never met. This woman stated, "It was just two different ways of looking at the world. As far as my husband is concerned, friendship is something that is mutually earned and is built up over a long period of increasing trust and openness. The ward, on the other hand, assumed that if enough people could give him an enthusiastic welcome, he would be won over. People meant well, but to him, these effusive welcomes were out of place and in poor taste. He felt that their real motive was missionary zeal—'Here's somebody we can grab for bap- tism.' " She commented further, "People kept saying to me the following Sunday, 'Oh, your husband seems like such a fine man. We'd like to get to know him better.' But it stopped there. They haven't made any effort to get to know him on a purely social basis, though it would mean a lot to me if we could trade dinner invitations with some of the other families in the ward."

Ward leaders as well as ward members need to be careful not to make assumptions about a nonmember or less-active husband's attitudes toward the organization and customs of the Church. One woman had been taught all her life that her bishop was someone she could turn to in difficult moments. When she and her husband were not able to resolve a discussion over whether they should uproot and move to a new location, it was natural to her to turn to her bishop for counsel, and her husband, who was not a Latter-day Saint, agreed to the meeting. Both the wife and the husband expected that the tone of the meeting would be that of a discussion among equals. Unfortunately, the bishop, though probably intending no offense whatever, spoke as one in authority not only over the Latter-day Saint woman but also over her non–Latter-day Saint husband. The husband's response afterward was, "What made him think he was entitled to tell me what to do?"

Like many women in nontraditional situations, women whose husbands are not Latter-day Saints or are less active gain an additional measure of compassion and understanding for those whose lives are complicated or problematical in some way. A friend said, "I'm determined to make my marriage work, but it's not easy. I was in love. I was naive. I didn't really know what it would mean to be devoted to the Church when the man I was married to wasn't. But I get a lot of satisfaction from being the one a lot of the women turn to when they need to talk about their problems to a sympathetic ear. I guess they realize that after what I've been through, I can really understand someone who doesn't fit the traditional Latter-day Saint mold."

CHAPTER SEVEN

The Woman Who Has It All but Is Still Unhappy

The women we have discussed so far have identifiable characteristics that distinguish them from the traditional Latter-day Saint wife-and-mother model. But what about the woman who appears to be right at the center, who has the blessings of home, family, and children, who has been active all her life in the Church, and who still feels like an outsider? She may say to herself, "I am so fortunate; I have my husband, I have my children, our health and finances are stable, and I know that so many women would envy my situation. I should be happy. Yet I'm not." This woman, too, feels like she does not belong. What is her place as an unhappy homemaker in a Church that supports her in her homemaking role, promises her joy in the fulfillment of it, and praises her for carrying it out? She does not feel satisfied, and she feels guilty for not having found the fulfillment that others appear to find in their callings as wives and mothers.

First Case History

Jennifer got married after one year at Brigham Young University. She then worked for three years while her husband finished his master's degree in public administration. He did not have a great number of job offers after he finished his degree, and they moved to Louisiana so that he could take advantage of the offer that seemed to be the best. Their first child was born just three months before they moved from Provo.

Both Jennifer and her husband were sad to move so far away from their families in Utah. They knew it was good for them to become more independent, for their parents to be further away than just a local phone call, but Jennifer had never felt so isolated. Even with two bedrooms, she felt their apartment was terribly cramped, especially when the papers, brief cases, and notebooks that symbolized her husband's conscientious nature — he brings work home every night — seemed to be piled up everywhere.

Her husband is a kind and responsible father, but he takes it for granted that both of them feel entirely comfortable with Jennifer assuming 98 percent of the child care. He doesn't ask whether Jennifer is happy. He just knows that they always planned to have children and that Jennifer always assumed she would be a mother, so he takes it as a given that she must be happy.

Two years ago, when their second baby was born, Jennifer went through a time of great frustration and exhaustion. The baby had colic, and for weeks the only time he was not crying was when he was nursing or asleep. Jennifer is the oldest of seven children, and she can't recall any of her brothers or sisters being so demanding and bad-tempered as her own two children. She remembers clearly that each new brother or sister who came along consumed a great deal of her mother's time, yet her mother seemed to move through the child-care responsibilities with great aplomb, not paying nearly the emotional price Jennifer feels she is paying. She feels that she has almost no life or identity of her own.

She promised herself long ago not to complain about her husband's long working hours, but she now finds it very difficult to keep that promise. Was it really necessary to his success for him to go to so many Chamber of Commerce mixers, fund-raisers, receptions? People are quite accustomed to seeing him alone at such functions; he just explains that Jennifer is "home with our babies." On those occasions when she makes a point of arranging for him to stay with the children so that she can attend a homemaking meeting or another Relief Society function, he usually replies, "Yes, I'll be glad to baby-sit that evening."

Baby-sit??? She has to bite her tongue. "These are your own children," she wants to tell him. "You don't *baby-sit* your own children! You tend them, you take care of them, but you don't baby-sit them."

A year ago they were able to buy their first home, so they are no longer so cramped for space. Jennifer has what she has always wanted—a home, a righteous and hard-working husband, and two children whom she dearly loves. Yet she feels unhappy. She does not think her husband has any idea of the effort it requires for her to provide the comforts he takes so much for granted. He has no idea, for instance, how time-consuming it is to go grocery shopping with two small children. He considers that the meals, the clean laundry, the clean home, are privileges he has earned because of the hard day he has put in at work. It does not occur to him that he collects these rewards at Jennifer's expense, not at his employer's expense.

As a single woman, Jennifer did not really think seriously about a career, because she had looked forward to being a wife and mother. But lately she has been reading the part-time employment opportunities in the classified ads section of the local newspaper. She feels that if she could get out of the house one or two days a week, be with other adults, and earn even a small amount of money, that would make all the difference in the way she feels about herself. But she has not even mentioned the subject to her husband. She knows what would happen if she did. First he would be baffled at the notion that she was not happy staying with her children in her new home, and then he would proceed to show her mathematically that it would actually *cost* money for her to work part-time by the time child-care expenses were figured in.

She feels especially guilty about her growing resentment every time she hears a priesthood holder say things like, "You mothers in Zion are truly blessed. There could be no happier, more joyful calling." "You haven't tried it," she can't help muttering to herself. She loves her children and her husband and would not trade them for anything, but she doesn't want to hear about the "happiness" she should feel, especially from someone who has not experienced the personal cost exacted by those very same blessings.

Second Case History

By far the brightest one in her family, Rayla was the pride of her small Wyoming town from the time she was a young girl because of the way she distinguished herself as a writer and a student of literature. She is proud of that reputation. She has been writing roadshows, skits, and talks since she was thirteen, and her work has been published several times in the Church magazines. She also wrote the lyrics to a song that won first place in one of the Church contests. She earned a master's degree in English, and after only five years of high school English teaching, she achieved a reputation as one of the finest English teachers in the state. Her students loved her.

When she was twenty-eight years old, she fell in love and was married. Rayla and Frank did not want to postpone a family, and Rayla took a mischievous delight in pointing out to people that their first baby was due nine months and one day after the wedding.

They loved their new baby and boasted constantly of his good looks and achievements. "You sound more like grand-parents than parents," one friend commented. But with the arrival of more children — there would be five in all — she began to feel discouraged at times about her role as a mother. After a lifetime of successes and honors, she often feels like a failure.

What does she mean by failure? Well, no one who came to Rayla's home and met her family would consider her a failure. But in her previous career, Rayla could feel a sense of satisfaction and closure at the end of a semester in seeing that most of her students had moved from a lower point to a higher point in their appreciation and skills. And now, what has she accomplished during any given day? She has nursed the baby six times, tried to take a nap in coordination with the baby's nap to recover from lost sleep the night before, and made at least some effort to take care of her house. So much of what she does is quickly undone, just in the normal course of family life: clean clothes are quickly dirty again, a neat house turns into a messy one in no time at all, and a meal is quickly consumed, leaving only dirty dishes and the prospect of fixing the *next* meal in a few hours.

Perhaps the hardest thing of all is that not one of Rayla's children is anything but a mediocre student. The three oldest children grudgingly take music lessons, but devouring junk food, "hanging out" with their friends, shopping at the mall, and constantly listening to meaningless popular music seem to be their chief interests. She is still hoping things will be different with the younger two.

Contrast these children with what she had pictured when she and Frank first talked of having a family: children just as eager as she had been as a child to read each new book, hear each new piece of music; and these children would have the advantage of Rayla for a mother, someone who would share, teach, and inspire. She had so much to offer them as a mother, so much knowledge and enthusiasm that would bring them a world of joy, and yet what they accepted from her they could just as well accept from any robot who could fix the meals and do the laundry.

To Rayla's frustration, her husband seems content with things as they are. The children are healthy, and they are staying out of major trouble. Although he was an excellent student and a voracious reader as a young man, his philosophy is just to "let the kids be themselves and appreciate them for what they are." He has virtually no empathy for Rayla's disappointment and unhappiness as a mother, and on those occasions when he has come home to find her in tears, his response has been wry and rueful. He even speaks in the third person instead of directly to her, as if he is reflecting out loud rather than offering comfort: "Poor dear. The responsibilities of motherhood weigh heavily upon her."

A friend told her, "Rayla, your kids aren't an extension of you. Do what you want; don't live through them. Let them shift for themselves a little more. You aren't going to change your kids or your husband." At this friend's invitation, she joined a women's issues discussion group, made up of Latter-day Saint and non–Latter-day Saint women. Rayla had been interested in topics relating to women for many years. When she taught high school, in fact, she was known as someone who could inspire the high school girls to plan to develop their talents and take advantage of their opportunities. But after three meetings of the discussion group, she decided not to attend any longer. The topics were interesting, and she liked most of the women, but they didn't seem to accept most of her comments as valid. After all, she was a traditional wife and mother with children, a nice home, and a husband who supported her financially. What did she know about women's struggles when no man had ever "done her wrong"?

One day she read a book review that mentioned the large number of recent novels that treated the theme of "the divided life." "That's me," Rayla thought. "I go to church, I hear the talks and lessons, people think of me as Sister Smith with that nice husband and those five children. I smile, I attend my meetings. They have no idea how different my thinking is — how unhappy I am. I'm not whole. I do live a divided life."

In Geoffrey Chaucer's "Wife of Bath's Tale," one of the *Canterbury Tales,* a knight is required to solve a riddle: "What do women most desire?" (He spends a year hunting for the answer, by the way, and when he finds it, the answer perhaps tells more about the character of the feisty and energetic Wife of Bath than it does about women in general. The answer he finds is that women want to be the boss in marriage!)

Many Latter-day Saints feel confident that they could answer this riddle quite easily for the Latter-day Saint woman: a temple marriage to a righteous and responsible bread-winner, children, and a lovely home. But many women can attest that even when they have these wonderful blessings, and even when they know they would make the same de-cisions again if they could turn back the clock, they still can

91

face times (sometimes long ones) of low morale, low self-esteem, and depression. Here is the way Salt Lake City psychiatrist Libby R. Hirsh describes the problem:

"Let us postulate a prospective Patti Perfect. Patti Jr. has been born and raised in Tinytown, Utah. Her father is the bishop of her ward, her mother is the Relief Society president, and her uncle down the block is the stake president. Patti's small town is approximately 98 percent Mormon, and she has never really learned to understand that there are other people on this earth who exist without the influence of the gospel in their lives. Patti has been raised to believe that anything a bishop, stake president, even a Relief Society board member, may say (on *any* subject, mind you) is absolute gospel truth. Patti's entire life plan has been made for her since at least the age of three when she first learned to say 'celestial.' She will graduate from high school and will have a husband in the wings or, in lieu thereof, will continue on at BYU (not particularly to learn or develop a talent or career, but to find the elusive returned missionary who will take her to the temple, place her on a pedestal, and provide her total security in life). She will marry, have six children, and carry at least four high positions in the Church. And she will live happily ever after. Now you can imagine in this plan what innumerable pitfalls and traps have been set. Patti has learned to define herself and her life in terms of attributes or events totally outside her control. Patti believes that if she does not marry, she must be unworthy and a failure. If she marries, has her six children, but then feels unhappy, she will experience a major loss in terms of unfulfilled expectations; she will, however, worsen her own situation by believing that because she feels this, she is guilty. The 'Church' has promised her that these things will make her happy, and surely if she is not, the fault is hers; an underlying *sin* must be preventing her progression."

("Being Well Balanced," *Woman to Woman,* Salt Lake City: Deseret Book Co., 1986, pp. 164–65.)

So it's not just the unhappiness; it's the guilt over feeling unhappy. A woman does not feel challenged in her domestic role, does not feel fulfilled by it, and does not feel recognized for it. Yet it seems to be enough for other women, so the problem must lie with her. She is the outsider.

Most Mormon women can relate to these frustrations. We wish we could prove ourselves through some dramatic, courageous deed. The call comes to gather to Jackson County, let's say, and without a second's hesitation we drop everything and set out to march with the faithful to Missouri. Unfortunately, next Monday is not nearly as likely to bring a call to gather to Missouri as it is to bring a pile of dirty laundry that we are expected to take care of. Most of life — especially the life of a mother — is made up of unrewarding, repetitious tasks.

I do not pretend that I have paid all my dues in this category, because I have not had the responsibility of rearing young children. But I have done a lot of observing and discussing, and during the time I have been married and have shared the responsibility for a teenager, I have gained some insights into this dilemma. I have stood by the dryer, pairing the clean socks, and said to myself, "I am over-qualified for this job." How is it possible to keep morale high when the tasks you must repeat are usually unexciting and often unappreciated? Perhaps if there were some way of being recognized — if motherhood carried with it a really impressive weekly paycheck, or if trophies were given out to the woman who remembered to go through *every* jeans pocket on laundry day for ten years, or if the entire nation could see a coast-to-coast instant replay of the brilliant way in which you handled your toddler's impending tantrum in the grocery store — the job of motherhood would carry considerable satisfaction.

93

In the meantime, here are some mental aerobics that may help you to feel more "up" about the work you carry out in your home.

1. *Give yourself full credit for what you do.* No law says you are not entitled to feel proud — even to gloat — when you handle a difficult situation well or when you see the results of your unsung heroism show up here and there. When something goes well, allow yourself to bask in your achievements.

Some women do a much better job than others of "collecting on their paydays." A friend of mine said, "A while ago we had a family home evening that really went well. I said to myself, 'Well, there would be more *novelty* in skiing down the slopes at Aspen, and it would be really *exciting* to be eating dinner at Maxim's in Paris, but the fact is that I couldn't be anyplace else, with anyone else, that would make me happier than being right here right now.' " She was collecting on a payday. Her lovely family was in large measure the result of her work and dedication, and she was allowing herself to enjoy that fact.

Another woman had just finished making a senior prom dress for her daughter. While other families had spent small fortunes on dresses for their daughters, she had made this one for under forty dollars, and most important, her daughter — a rather temperamental and choosy girl — was thrilled with the dress. She watched her daughter leave for the evening, looking beautiful, and then her mind immediately leaped ahead to her responsibilities for a dinner for a huge family reunion that would be happening in only two weeks. She stopped herself suddenly: "Wait a second. I have just scored a major triumph through my dedication and creativity. What's wrong with me that I can't allow at least a few minutes just to enjoy this achievement before I begin to fuss over something else?" This woman has now adopted a custom of giving herself a pat on the back (when no one is looking) each time she does something especially noteworthy. When she's especially pleased with herself, she says that it's quite a "slug between the shoulderblades." It's her private symbol, just her way, of ensuring that she takes a brief moment to give herself credit — that she collects on her payday.

Collecting on one's payday is not a matter of saying, "As soon as I finish this batch of ironing, I'll treat myself to a Hershey's Golden Almond." It's a matter of saying, "It's tough, but I've done it, and I'm proud." One friend of mine makes a list each morning of what she is going to do that day. She has an excellent memory, and she certainly doesn't need a list to remind her what to do, especially when the list includes such items as "fix lunch." But she *loves* crossing them off! Each line that she draws through an item is a minor payday, and at the end of the day, it's a long list of achievements that helps her feel she has really been productive.

2. *Don't measure your contribution by false financial yardsticks.* When a homemaker begins to think, "What am I really worth?" it is a temptation to sit down and compute the actual market value of her activities on an average day: for instance, eight hours at the going rate for child care, two hours of housecleaning at so many dollars an hour, and so forth.

There are two problems with this kind of figuring. First of all, the rates for these activities are usually not very high, so the total theoretical "replacement cost," if she were not there to carry out these activities, is demoralizingly low.

The second problem, and by far the more important, is that the market value of household tasks is not a true measure of their worth. My friend Kathleen Slaugh (now Kathleen Bahr) decided as a graduate student to study the unseen values of housework and the result was a Ph.D. dissertation

titled "Family Interaction and Human Resource Develop-
ment in the Housework Context." She obtained permission
from several families to observe them in their homes while
making herself as invisible as possible. In this way she was
able to study what she called the "socialization function" of
housework, noting that housework has the potential to bring
families together in a repeated, purposeful way that has many
results besides the housework itself. Under a somewhat
friendlier title, "More than Clean Windows," she summa-
rized a few of her findings in the October 1985 *Ensign:*

"Reducing the value of housework to its market equiv-
alents focuses our attention on the products of our labor—
the washed dish, the vacuumed house, the bathed child. But
these products are secondary. The more important value of
these tasks lies in the social situations in which they take
place. . . . Many parents have reported reaching a level of
intimacy in such settings that is difficult, if not impossible,
to achieve under more formal conditions. Children sense
their contribution to family goals is needed and appreciated.
Working together at humble tasks can dissolve barriers between parents and children and bring greater feelings of
unity."

So it is important to remember that a person hired to
do the same tasks—fix a meal, for example, or care for
children—does not really achieve the same results, even
though the meal may be fine and the children kept safe and
happy. The context of housework gives a family an opportunity for sharing, teaching, joking, planning, in a way that
no other situation does. One friend of mine complained,
several years ago when her children were very young, "I
never have time to teach them anything!" In her mind,
"teaching" meant lining her little girls up in a row and
delivering a lesson. Kathleen Slaugh's study emphasizes that
my friend was *constantly* teaching her children—teaching

them very important things, in fact. The very same routine tasks that supposedly left her no time for teaching carried the most important lessons of all. These lessons by their nature are abstract and subliminal, lessons taught more effectively by example than by precept. Instead of having to do with numbers, colors, letters, and shapes, they had to do with attitudes, planning, social skills, cleanliness, the handling of happy moments and sad moments. Household tasks, then, add up to much more than their market value.

If you still wish to link your domestic labors to a financial figure, here is a much better way to approach the question: what would you require as an annual salary to do exactly the same work, but for a group of strangers? What would you charge, in other words, to do exactly the same planning, worrying, cooking, laundry, cleaning, disciplining, transporting, and so forth, for a group of people that you had no emotional connection with?

Several times, when I have given talks in front of groups of Latter-day Saint women, I have asked for someone from the audience to volunteer to answer this question. The lowest figure any woman has ever named was fifty thousand dollars, which the rest of the women in the audience thought was somewhat low. The highest was half a million dollars, and the woman who named this figure was totally serious. She was simply not willing to do this exhausting, endless work for a lesser amount, and she made it clear that this was for one year only; she would then retire on the interest income from her half-million dollars!

In the corporate world, some salaries reach this half-million dollar mark or even higher. That young mother's answer was really not so far out of line. What does someone do to earn such a huge salary? These salaries are paid for experience, long hours, dedication, a whole variety of skills — requirements familiar to every homemaker. And to this list we should add "exposure." Exposure means that part of the reason for the large salary is that if this person makes a mistake, the consequences are widespread and serious. Although most families do a good job of absorbing small mistakes and carrying on just fine, a mother does not want to make significant, long-term mistakes. On the large-scale questions — the questions of what kind of relationship is she able to establish with her family members, and what kind of atmosphere is she able to create in her home — there is little room for error.

3. *Don't make meaningless comparisons.* When you see that lovely, smiling family walking together into church before the meeting starts, it is easy to forget that you are seeing their *public* face. You have no idea of the work and conflict and tensions that might have preceded this impressive arrival at the church. We tend to evaluate others in terms of their best moments. To think, "Why can't my family be like *that* one?" is discouraging and unfair.

Every family struggles; every family pays its dues. On those rare occasions when we talk about this fact openly, it can bring a lot of comfort. My husband came home from priesthood meeting not long ago and related that one of the men, an outstanding husband and father whose family is admired and respected by all, decided to make a frank comment in their priesthood class discussion on family home evening. He said, "In my house, family home evening is the only fight that opens and closes with prayer." Where-upon another equally prominent and respected man responded, "Well, in *my* house, family prayer is the only prayer that opens and closes with a fight!" The rest of the quorum laughed and breathed a real sigh of relief, of course. These very open comments helped each man to realize, "Maybe my family isn't so different after all."

Comparisons with other families are not the only kinds

of comparisons that may be harmful. All around us are false pictures of what life supposedly can be. Part of growing up is realizing that the characters and families we see in movies and on television or read about in romantic fiction have virtually nothing to do with real life. But how many women lose themselves in a novel about a gorgeous and witty (and probably titled) young heroine who is swept off her feet and carried off to a castle by a mysterious and handsome stranger? Then they put the book down with a sigh and think, "My life's not like that!" Indeed not! Life never has been like that—not today and certainly not back in the days of Lady Clarissa or whoever that fictional heroine is. Nor can the problems of life be solved in thirty minutes minus commercials, the way our favorite television families solve them.

We tend to overrate other people's happiness; we tend to idealize other people's roles and activities. The life of a well-dressed career woman who gets her hair and nails done twice a week may seem so enviable to a mother who feels confined at home with her young children. But there's a truism that's worth remembering: every job has its dirty diapers. Every career woman has known pangs of envy when she sees a mother's joy in her family. It's human nature to think, "Someone else is happier and better off." We can hold up ideals that will increase our righteous conduct and our happiness, but we should be sure they are valid spiritual ideals, not superficial comparisons from some other source.

Homemakers do thankless things, over and over, year after year, in a divine cause: the welfare of those they love. The best scripture I know to validate these enduring efforts is from Alma 37:6–7: "Behold I say unto you, that by small and simple things are great things brought to pass; . . . and by very small means the Lord doth confound the wise and bringeth about the salvation of many souls."

CHAPTER EIGHT

Surrounded by Sisterhood

Within the scope of this book it is not possible to talk about every kind of false barrier that may seem to divide Latter-day Saint women from one another. It is not just our marital status, our family situation, or our past lives that may threaten our association and understanding; other factors may pose problems or even seem like total barriers to full and joyful activity in the Church.

What are some of the other differences that might cause a woman to hesitate to enter fully into the program of the Church? The list is a long one. Here are a few that come to mind:

1. A woman's educational level may be different — either higher or lower — from the typical level in her group, and she may sense that she has less acceptance from the other women or less in common with them.

2. Her financial situation may set her apart from others in the group. She may feel embarrassed because she is on a tight budget, or she may worry that she is the target of resentment because she is financially better off than the others.

3. She may be a mother who works outside the home when most of the other women in the ward are not employed, or a full-time homemaker in a ward where many are employed outside the home. For some women, the morale boost of working outside the home helps them be more energetic and good-natured as mothers; for others, working drains them of energy and makes them bad-tempered at home. Energies and circumstances can vary widely.

4. She may be too glamorous to gain easy credibility when she moves into a new ward. (We should all have such problems!)

5. She may be near one end or the other of the adult age spectrum. How does a single eighteen-year-old relate to a Relief Society discussion on child-rearing? How does a ninety-four-year-old relate to a discussion of the Word of Wisdom, when she feels fairly confident by now that she is not going to die young from smoking too much?

6. A woman may be from another country, with cultural and language barriers to be overcome. Even moving from state to state within the United States can mean tremendous and often unsuspected cultural differences.

7. Physical handicaps may limit activity; even when the handicapped woman does not feel limited, other women may feel unsure and awkward when dealing with her, especially if she is new in the ward.

8. A woman's household may not fall even within the definition of *household* that includes single parents and blended families. The household may be an extended-family home that includes fairly distant relatives, or it may be a household in which two or more unrelated women share a home. It is interesting to note that only 19 percent of Latter-day Saint households meet all three requirements of the traditional picture of the ideal household: (1) a husband and wife who are (2) married in the temple and have (3)

children living at home. (See Kristen L. Goodman and Tim B. Heaton, "LDS Church Members in the U. S. and Canada: A Demographic Profile," *AMCAP Journal,* vol. 12 no. 1, 1986, p. 96.)

9. Latter-day Saint women are known for their domestic skills. If a woman feels incompetent when it comes to baking, needlework, and so forth, she may feel genuinely embarrassed and out of place around other women whom she perceives as more competent.

10. The responsibility of caring for a handicapped or elderly family member may take so great a toll on a woman's time and resources that her Church activities, friendships, and outside interests may all be curtailed.

And this list does not even begin to exhaust the many individual circumstances that may be found within the boundaries of one ward or branch. Nevertheless, we can live our distinctive lives and still be one—still feel comfortable around one another, have a sense of acceptance and support. Whose responsibility is it to establish these ties, to make sure that women of every background and circumstance have an opportunity to feel welcome in the ward? Who should build these bridges?

Throughout this book I have tried not to place the burden of responsibility on either the group or the individual woman, because it does not belong exclusively to either. It can work both ways. Sometimes the "outsider woman" must stop worrying about being an outsider and instead begin to exercise patience and initiative to be accepted by a group that may not be as alert and receptive as it should; sometimes the group must do everything but turn cartwheels to convince the woman who feels like an outsider that if she joins in with the ward activities she will find friends, interests, and support.

What a challenge for a visiting teacher! With prayer and

imagination, she must seek to custom fit her visit and her message to each individual sister she is assigned to teach, to relate to each sister's strengths and problems in a unique and meaningful way. A sensitive visiting teacher will give a different emphasis to the message and leave a different challenge in each home because she knows and appreciates the individuality of each woman she visits.

What about the woman who may have achieved a considerable degree of acceptance in a ward but then must start all over again when she moves to another ward? My family and I have moved three times in the last two years—to a different stake in California, to Texas, and then back to California. In the process I've learned some pointers that will help a woman give herself every advantage as she seeks to feel comfortable in a new ward and to help others feel comfortable around her. Some of these suggestions are major, some are minor, but each one will help to shorten the time between her arrival and her full-fledged association.

1. Remember that even though you may feel like the only outsider, you are surrounded by women who feel the same way to a greater or lesser degree. Remember Claudia Bushman's statement: "[Most Church members] think some wonderful hidden life is going on without them. I'd estimate that the majority of faithful Church members feel out of it for not measuring up to some idea or other while, on the other hand, some of those who feel most secure have little reason to be so, when measured by the same requirements. I often feel 'out of it' myself, and who is more in it than I?" "A Celebration of Sisterhood," *Dialogue,* Summer 1987, p. 134.)

2. Keep the Word of Wisdom.

3. Attend ward social functions as well as Sunday meetings.

4. Be prepared to contribute, even if assignments and

callings are personally disappointing. There is an expression—"Church-broke"—that has nothing to do with housebreaking a pet. It is related instead to the cowboy expression "saddle-broke." A horse that has accepted the saddle and will be loyal and trustworthy from then on is "saddle-broke." In much the same way, a "Church-broke" woman will not allow personal offenses or discouragement to interfere with her loyalty to the Church and its organizations. If someone fails to credit you for an assignment you have carried out, if someone dents your car in the parking lot and fails to leave a note, if an insensitive person is overcritical of you or a family member, resolve to carry on anyway in true, "Church-broke" fashion.

5. If parts of the routine are uncomfortable or unfamiliar, pick out a pleasant and nonjudgmental sister and ask for help. For example, if you dread being called on to offer a prayer in Relief Society, ask a sister to meet with you to talk over some of the things that are usually included in such a prayer so that you can feel more comfortable when you are asked.

6. Don't feel accountable; don't feel you must explain every detail of your past and present life. Your present desire to join in with your sisters and your ward, to render service, to reap the blessings, is all that really counts. If you are the target of tactless curiosity, try to set an example of courtesy in return, but don't feel that you have to answer all questions. If you wish to clarify something about your situation once and for all (for example, that your husband will not be attending meetings with you, or that you are divorced from the father of your children), you may wish to take the initiative and volunteer that information. In any case, don't let the inevitable questions take you by surprise. Plan the answers you feel the most comfortable with.

7. Be ready to give and accept good will. Assume the best.

These suggestions describe what the outsider can do to belong more readily. As we've acknowledged earlier, ward members have a responsibility too. A ward that is good at welcoming newcomers can help you assimilate, but at least half the task rests in your hands. The productive place to spend your time and emotional energies is in ensuring your friendliness, your willingness, and your openness to new associations, rather than worrying about seemingly unfriendly ward members. It is impossible for me to think that a reasonable and well-intentioned woman who follows these suggestions would not find herself welcome in a ward or branch anywhere in the Church.

Individuality is a precious gift from our Heavenly Father, one that we all prize. No one is a clone of anyone else, and in that respect each of us can enjoy being unlike all the other women. But once in a while we will find a woman who paradoxically seems to enjoy the negative aspects of being an outsider. Anger generates the steam that fuels her life; she looks for reasons to feel slighted and passed over; she takes note of each lesson or activity that is not aimed at individuals in her particular situation. She is like the woman in Robert Burns's "Tam O'Shanter,"

> *Gathering her brows like a gathering storm,*
> *Nursing her wrath to keep it warm.*

(*British Literature 1800 to the Present,* vol. 2, ed. Hazelton Spencer et al., Lexington, Mass.: D. C. Heath and Co., 1974, p. 47.)

A woman like the one Burns describes "keeps her wrath warm" by feeling victimized and misunderstood. Sister Norma B. Ashton offers some excellent advice, quoting her husband, Elder Marvin J. Ashton:

"My husband often says, 'Never let yourself be offended by someone who is learning his job.' Because we are a lay church and because we all change jobs at what seem to be brief intervals, we are all constantly learning how to fulfill new assignments. No one should ever let himself be hurt by a brother or sister in the gospel. We are each too worthy to be upset by someone else." ("For Such a Time As This, the Time Is Now," *Woman to Woman,* Salt Lake City: Deseret Book Co., 1986, p. 18.)

Obviously, ward members can do some things to make newcomers' arrival much more comfortable. My own ward Relief Society president has stressed to her board that it is the responsibility of every board member to mix and mingle, to look around at each meeting or social event, and identify new sisters or those who may need a friendly word. We have revised our "Relief Society Information Card" that we hand to move-ins on their first Sunday. The old one looked like this:

Name: Address: Phone: Husband's Name: Husband's Priesthood: Children's names and ages: Callings you have held:

The new card yields all the same information, but it looks like this:

WELCOME TO RELIEF SOCIETY!   Please give us the following information so we can get to know you better: Name: Address: Phone:

If any of the following information is relevant, please include it:
  Husband's name:
  Priesthood:
  Children's names and ages:
  Callings you have held:

The changes are fairly minor, but the unstated messages are quite different, and new converts, unmarried women, or those married to men who are not Latter-day Saints can feel much more welcome on their first day in the ward.

An alert ward leader will know that the new arrival may bring just the talents or insights their group has been needing. Louise Plummer, in a delightful *Ensign* article called "Thoughts of a Grasshopper," writes, "I've always wondered if there is room in a family of ants — or in a church of ants — for a grasshopper. I fear that ants will not accept me unless I am just like them." She suggests a new ending for Aesop's fable of the grasshopper and the ants. Instead of the ants telling the grasshopper, "You sang through the summer, now you can dance through the winter," she has created her own ending, one that places proper value on the grasshopper's talents:

"It is winter and the grasshopper is walking in the snow, talking to herself and answering herself. She wears a yellow slicker over her sweater because she can't find her parka (which is buried in the debris under her bed). Because she was out of groceries this morning, she is eating a brownie with a carton of milk bought at the local convenience store which, thank heaven, is open twenty-four hours a day. The door in the tree where the ants live swings open. The queen ant appears and says to the grasshopper, 'We are bored to death. Won't you tell us a story or at least a good joke? Our teenagers are driving us crazy; maybe you could write them a play to perform, or just a roadshow? Do you have any ideas for a daddy-daughter party?'

"The grasshopper replies that she has ideas for all of them. So the ant invites her in and seats her at a spotless kitchen table with pencil and paper, and the grasshopper writes the roadshow.

"The ant feeds her guest a slice of homemade bread, fresh from the oven, and a glass of freshly squeezed orange juice. 'How do you get all of these ideas?' she asks the grasshopper.

" 'They come to me,' says the grasshopper, 'while I am taking long hot baths.' " (Aug. 1988, p. 71.)

It is important to remember that the typical bishop has had no firsthand experiences in any of the circumstances we have discussed. If he got married soon after his mission, he has never, for all practical purposes, been single. He may well be a lifelong, active Latter-day Saint, with no firsthand knowledge of what it is like to leave behind a sinful or "drop-out" life and rejoin the fold; he has probably not been a single parent; he is almost certainly not married to a non-member; he probably does not have a blended family; he probably has not been divorced. If he seems insensitive in deeds or actions, remember Sister Norma Ashton's advice: "Never let yourself be offended by someone learning his job." Because he has not encountered these situations himself, he is still learning to understand them. Be patient.

Many people may not have the patience, the imagination, or the empathy to see the world through the eyes of someone else. To these people, no one else's lives or problems are very real, and no one significantly different from themselves can be a good Latter-day Saint. Such people can become more sensitive, of course, but in the meantime they are more likely to express blame or bafflement than understanding.

Everyone at some time feels isolated or excluded. Everyone at some time feels as if she is criticized for not con-
forming to certain norms, even though the world may be
measuring her by yardsticks that are not relevant to her life,
her talents, or her responsibilities. Judgments and misun-
derstandings are rife. Only our Father in Heaven is qualified
to judge, yet many people are in the habit of constantly
judging. The waves of public opinion may come so unex-
pectedly and with such force that it may require every ounce
of personal strength to keep from drowning!

Each of us can make a personal resolution: "I will not
contribute to speculative, critical, and irresponsible public
opinion. I will respect the motives and choices of other
women. As someone who does not know all the trials someone else may have gone through or all the pressures she
may be facing, I will decline to judge. I will make every
effort to understand, appreciate, and encourage. I realize
that most women are handling their lives in the best way
they know how. I will not make things more difficult for
them by judging."

If you find yourself starting to say or think any of these
things, stop yourself immediately:

1. I wonder why she's never married.

2. I wonder what she does with herself all day.

3. She should have realized that when she married him.

4. If they couldn't have any children of their own, at least
they should have adopted some.

5. They are such a great couple. They should just get
back together and patch things up.

6. If she had spent more time with her children, she
would have seen these problems coming.

7. If he left her, he must have had a reason.

8. I wonder why she doesn't just pull herself together.

9. They should have more [or fewer] children.

10. I know she's passed up opportunities to get married.

11. She has so many problems in her life; she must not be very close to the Lord.

12. You'd think she would have learned her lesson.

13. I wonder why she has so many friends outside the Church and so few inside.

14. I wish she would realize that _____ is a job for [a man, a younger woman, etc.].

15. I wonder why they haven't had more children.

16. It's time they stopped having children.

17. It's terrible that she's pregnant again so soon.

18. I think her health problems are mostly in her mind.

19. She says she needs _____, but she really needs _____.

20. Obviously, they must have made some mistakes as parents.

21. It's ridiculous for her to keep hoping for _____.

22. Why doesn't she take better care of herself and lose/gainsome weight?

23. How could she put her own mother in a nursing home?

24. She should just put her mother in a nursing home.

25. On her budget, _____ is too much of an extravagance.

Many women, without fanfare, manage to deal with extremely difficult circumstances in their health, their home situation, their employment, and other aspects of their lives. The outside world may see the woman mainly as the mother of an often troublesome teenager, or as someone who does not attend most of her meetings; yet to achieve even the result of keeping the teenager halfway under control or to attend even a few meetings may be the result of real heroism behind the scenes. It is inappropriate to be critical. We are better off if we judge not.

A home can take many different forms. Among the households of members of the Church are many types other than the one that is traditionally pictured as the Mormon ideal. A woman whose household is of a kind that is in the minority should remember that her minority is probably not so small after all. Following is a summary of the 1981 demographic study we have referred to several times. It is clear that no

COMPOSITION OF LDS HOUSEHOLDS

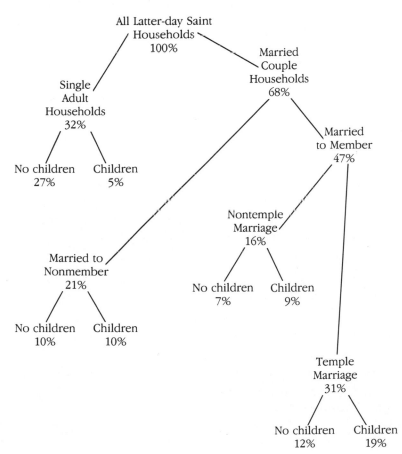

one type of household predominates among Latter-day Saints. Throughout the Church, faithful members are striving to establish gospel-centered homes under widely varying circumstances. We must stop defining *home* according to who lives there and instead focus our concern on what happens there. Is there sharing, support, a happy atmosphere, respect for individuality, a teaching and exemplifying of gospel principles? If so — or if the members of that household are sincerely striving toward those goals — then it is a home, whether it is a home with only one person living in it or a huge household that extends itself to include even nonrelatives.

Many of us have had the experience of bringing a friend or neighbor who was not a Latter-day Saint to a Relief Society function and suddenly realizing that the title "Sister," which we take for granted, to our friend might sound somewhat quaint at best and downright strange at worst. The "brothering and sistering" in our church is an old-fashioned custom, to be sure, but the great advantage of the title "Sister" is that it is totally egalitarian. Sisters are equal; the title by itself doesn't even hint which one may be the "big sister" or the "little sister." It refers to the woman herself, not to whether she is married or unmarried. It doesn't convey professional rank, church calling, or college degrees. So "Sister" as a form of address carries within it a significant, symbolic message: we are equals, working side by side, doing our best in our individual ways to build the kingdom. As sisters we can strengthen ourselves and each other. As sisters we can find unity in our diversity. As sisters we can thrive on our differences.

Index